DAYS OF
INFAMY

ALSO BY LAWRENCE GOLDSTONE

SEPARATE NO MORE: THE LONG ROAD TO
BROWN V. BOARD OF EDUCATION

STOLEN JUSTICE: THE STRUGGLE FOR
AFRICAN AMERICAN VOTING RIGHTS

UNPUNISHED MURDER: MASSACRE AT
COLFAX AND THE QUEST FOR JUSTICE

DAYS OF
INFAMY

HOW A CENTURY OF BIGOTRY LED TO
JAPANESE AMERICAN INTERNMENT

LAWRENCE GOLDSTONE

SCHOLASTIC
FOCUS
NEW YORK

This book includes quoted material from primary source documents, some of which contains racially offensive language. These passages are presented in their original, unedited form in order to accurately reflect history.

Library of Congress Cataloging-in-Publication Data Available

ISBN 978-1-338-72246-8

10 9 8 7 6 5 4 3 2 1   22 23 24 25 26

Printed in the U.S.A.   37

First edition, June 2022

Book design by Becky James

To Nancy, Lee, Tyler, and Patton

CONTENTS

PROLOGUE   xi

CHAPTER 1: Free and White   1

CHAPTER 2: White, Black, . . . and Gold   9

CHAPTER 3: Ah Yup   18

CHAPTER 4: Enter the Japanese   25

CHAPTER 5: Birthright   36

CHAPTER 6: Exclusion   45

CHAPTER 7: The Workers . . .   52

CHAPTER 8: . . . and the Boss   58

CHAPTER 9: Tremors   65

CHAPTER 10: A Convenient Target   77

CHAPTER 11: Mr. Schmitz Goes to Washington   84

CHAPTER 12: Here Come the Brides   93

CHAPTER 13: This Land Is (Not) Your Land   99

CHAPTER 14: Fake News   110

CHAPTER 15: Slamming the Golden Door   122

CHAPTER 16: All in the Family   129

CHAPTER 17: The Golden West   136

CHAPTER 18: The Heart of an American   147

CHAPTER 19: What Meets the Eye   164

CHAPTER 20: Turning the Soil   174

CHAPTER 21: Banzai and Baseball   181

CHAPTER 22: Fear and Fiction   190

CHAPTER 23: No Island Paradise   197

CHAPTER 24: Infamy   200

CHAPTER 25: Four Who Refused   210

EPILOGUE: Shame   224

BIBLIOGRAPHY   231

SOURCE NOTES   237

PHOTOGRAPH AND ILLUSTRATION CREDITS   249

INDEX   251

ACKNOWLEDGMENTS   263

ABOUT THE AUTHOR   265

DAYS OF
INFAMY

PROLOGUE

ON DECEMBER 8, 1941, one day after the Japanese navy launched an attack on American air and naval bases at Pearl Harbor in Oahu, Hawaii, President Franklin Roosevelt addressed a joint session of Congress. He told American lawmakers that December 7, 1941, was "a date which will live in infamy," and asked that a state of war be declared between the United States and Japan. While his denunciation of an unprovoked attack as the two nations were actively negotiating to resolve their differences was certainly justified, three years later, December 18, 1944, became another date that has lived in infamy, one about which President Roosevelt was silent. The reason for his lack of outrage on this occasion was perhaps because he was directly responsible for what would later be widely seen as an indelible stain on America's honor.

On that day, with the defeat of fascism glimmering into sight, the United States Supreme Court, by a 6–3 vote, ruled that the forced relocation of more than 100,000 Americans, two-thirds of whom were United States citizens, to what government officials themselves called "concentration camps," was fully justified under the United States Constitution. Not one of these Americans had been accused of a crime. They had been torn from their homes, jobs, schools, and communities to be deposited in tawdry, makeshift housing behind barbed wire solely because of their race.

President Roosevelt had authorized this action on February 19, 1942, with Executive Order 9066, which said effectively that anyone of Japanese heritage, citizen or not, was an "alien," a potential saboteur or enemy agent, and could thus have any rights guaranteed under the Constitution annulled in the name of national security. And so, the United States joined Fascist Italy and Nazi Germany as nations who forcibly deported citizens without trial simply because of the circumstances of their birth.

The case in which the Supreme Court upheld the same practice that America had condemned its enemies for, *Korematsu v. United States*, is now one of the few decisions in Supreme Court history that both liberals and conservatives list among the worst ever. In a blog on the legal website FindLaw, *Korematsu* was listed as the third worst decision ever, behind only *Dred Scott v. Sandford* and *Buck v. Bell* (where a Virginia teenager was sterilized against her will because she had been judged, incorrectly as it turned out, to be "feeble minded"), but ahead of such other travesties as *Plessy v. Ferguson* and *Citizens United v. Federal Election Commission*. To make the decision even more damning, the Court's two great champions of civil liberties, Hugo Black and William O. Douglas, voted with the majority. Black was the author of the opinion.

But as damning as *Korematsu* might have been, to tell the

WESTERN DEFENSE COMMAND AND FOURTH ARMY
WARTIME CIVIL CONTROL ADMINISTRATION

Presidio of San Francisco, California
April 1, 1942

INSTRUCTIONS
TO ALL PERSONS OF
JAPANESE
ANCESTRY

Living in the Following Area:

All that portion of the City and County of San Francisco, State of California, lying generally west of the north-south line established by Junipero Serra Boulevard, Worchester Avenue, and Nineteenth Avenue, and lying generally north of the east-west line established by California Street, to the intersection of Market Street, and thence on Market Street to San Francisco Bay.

All Japanese persons, both alien and non-alien, will be evacuated from the above designated area by 12:00 o'clock noon Tuesday, April 7, 1942.

No Japanese person will be permitted to enter or leave the above described area after 8:00 a. m., Thursday, April 2, 1942, without obtaining special permission from the Provost Marshal at the Civil Control Station located at:

1701 Van Ness Avenue
San Francisco, California

The Civil Control Station is equipped to assist the Japanese population affected by this evacuation in the following ways:

1. Give advice and instructions on the evacuation.

2. Provide services with respect to the management, leasing, sale, storage or other disposition of most kinds of property including: real estate, business and professional equipment, buildings, household goods, boats, automobiles, livestock, etc.

3. Provide temporary residence elsewhere for all Japanese in family groups.

4. Transport persons and a limited amount of clothing and equipment to their new residence, as specified below.

The Following Instructions Must Be Observed:

1. A responsible member of each family, preferably the head of the family, or the person in whose name most of the property is held, and each individual living alone, will report to the Civil Control Station to receive further instructions. This must be done between 8:00 a. m. and 5:00 p. m., Thursday, April 2, 1942, or between 8:00 a. m. and 5:00 p. m., Friday, April 3, 1942.

2. Evacuees must carry with them on departure for the Reception Center, the following property:

(a) Bedding and linens (no mattress) for each member of the family;

(b) Toilet articles for each member of the family;

(c) Extra clothing for each member of the family;

(d) Sufficient knives, forks, spoons, plates, bowls and cups for each member of the family;

(e) Essential personal effects for each member of the family.

All items carried will be securely packaged, tied and plainly marked with the name of the owner and numbered in accordance with instructions received at the Civil Control Station.

The size and number of packages is limited to that which can be carried by the individual or family group.

No contraband items as described in paragraph 6, Public Proclamation No. 3, Headquarters Western Defense Command and Fourth Army, dated March 24, 1942, will be carried.

3. The United States Government through its agencies will provide for the storage at the sole risk of the owner of the more substantial household items, such as iceboxes, washing machines, pianos and other heavy furniture. Cooking utensils and other small items will be accepted if crated, packed and plainly marked with the name and address of the owner. Only one name and address will be used by a given family.

4. Each family, and individual living alone, will be furnished transportation to the Reception Center. Private means of transportation will not be utilized. All instructions pertaining to the movement will be obtained at the Civil Control Station.

Go to the Civil Control Station at 1701 Van Ness Avenue, San Francisco, California, between 8:00 a. m. and 5:00 p. m., Thursday, April 2, 1942, or between 8:00 a. m. and 5:00 p. m., Friday, April 3, 1942, to receive further instructions.

J. L. DeWITT
Lieutenant General, U. S. Army
Commanding

SEE CIVILIAN EXCLUSION ORDER NO. 5

Poster ordering Japanese Americans to leave their homes and businesses.

story of the stigmatizing and imprisonment of thousands of innocent Americans as an isolated incident, a temporary loss of national purpose, would be to miss the point entirely. In fact, both the Court's decision and the events that preceded the case were simply the natural extensions of decades of blatant and unapologetic discrimination against men, women, and children whose only offense was to have Asian forebears. And the discrimination against these people did not begin because of acts of terrorism, but rather because they demonstrated a willingness to toil tirelessly for paltry recompense, absorb insult and abuse without complaint, and give up even the most meager luxury for the benefit of their children . . . all values that Americans claim to respect.

Nor were the justices unaware of the nature of the case before them. White supremacists in the West were as open in their intent to discriminate against Asian Americans as white supremacists in the South were willing to announce their intention to discriminate against African Americans. Law after law was passed to strangle immigration and to prevent those immigrants from Japan and China who were successful in entering the United States from becoming citizens. Further legislation then prevented Asian noncitizens from owning land, entering into real estate or commercial contracts, or enjoying constitutional protections afforded to most who lived within America's borders. Children of first-generation immigrants born in the United States, granted automatic citizenship by

Section 1 of the Fourteenth Amendment, were subject to other forms of discrimination designed to keep them separate from white Americans, measures that the Supreme Court had deemed constitutional in *Plessy v. Ferguson* in 1896.

Although all but a few thousand Japanese immigrants and citizens lived on the West Coast, the tensions between them and the white population had exploded into a national issue decades before the attack on Pearl Harbor. In January 1921, for example, a prestigious academic journal, *The Annals of the American Academy of Political and Social Science*, published in Philadelphia, devoted an entire issue to "Present-Day Immigration with Special Reference to the Japanese." There were twenty-three articles from such diverse contributors as the openly—and proudly—racist United States senator and former mayor of San Francisco, James D. Phelan, to Baron Shimpei Goto (now Gotō Shinpei), who had been the Japanese minister for foreign affairs. The arguments on both sides were almost identical to those that would appear twenty years later.

Baron Goto asserted that the Japanese in California "live very plainly and work very industrially and fulfill a useful and, I should say, almost unreplaceable function in the economic life of the state. Their honesty is unimpeachable, so much so that I have often heard it said that banks will advance them money on the conditions which (if proposed by Americans), will be refused. They are, of course, entirely peaceful." Senator Phelan, on the other hand, in an article titled, "Why California

Objects to the Japanese Invasion," called for Congress to act immediately on the "Japanese problem" and that "we admire their industry and cleverness, but for that very reason, being a masterful people, they are more dangerous." Phelan went on, "The people of Asia have a destiny of their own. We shall aid them by instruction and example, but we cannot suffer them to overwhelm the civilization which has been established by pioneers and patriots and which we are dutifully bound to preserve." Then in words that could easily have been uttered in 2019 about other races, Phelan said, "We are willing to receive diplomats, scholars and travelers from Japan on terms of equality, but we do not want her laborers."

Another critic, John S. Chambers, the California state controller, insisted, "Assimilation is impossible," and compared the Japanese to rodents. "Watch the gopher at work. He starts to bore into a levee, and as he progresses, he is joined by more of his kind; then, in due time, the other side of the embankment is reached, and a little stream of water passes through. As the dirt crumbles, a flow increases and unless promptly checked, the bore soon becomes a wide gap with the water rushing through and overflowing the land. That is the flood that means loss, and perhaps eventual disaster. That is exactly what is happening in the state of California today through the Japanese policy of peaceful penetration."

During the next two decades, however, many Japanese people not only assimilated, but also showed every sign of becoming a vital and indispensable part of the economies of western states, which infuriated the anti-Japanese faction all the more. "An official report noted that by 1910, the Japanese produced about half of the entire amount of [Californian] agricultural products marketed. Their position was substantially the same as that of the Chinese except that the sector of agriculture which they occupied had grown to be very much more important than it had been at the time of the Chinese."

In the aftermath of Pearl Harbor, white supremacists had their opportunity. They were able to not only claim foresight for insisting the Japanese were a treacherous race, but also to finally persuade the government in Washington to take the sort of action they had been urging for decades. And so, more than 100,000 people were deported, their homes and businesses either seized or vandalized, and in many cases, their lives ruined forever.

The story of the bigotry, prejudice, and oppression foisted on Americans of Japanese ancestry for almost half a century by individuals, government officials, and justices of the Supreme Court is one that resonates today. "White supremacy," the banner under which these injustices were perpetrated, not only to those of Asian heritage, but to Black and brown people, and Indigenous Americans as well, has been revived, not simply as an outlook hidden in the shadows, but as one that many are willing, even proud, to proclaim publicly.

And so, the United States government's treatment of the

Japanese is also a story of today's America, and the lessons of that terrible period in our history are lessons the nation cannot be allowed to forget. Although to combat bigotry and discrimination is the job of every American, the Supreme Court will once again be the venue where racism is either accepted or rejected in American law.

CHAPTER 1

FREE AND WHITE

THE UNITED STATES CONSTITUTION makes no mention of citizenship. Excluding enslaved people and "Indians not paying taxes"—who were assumed to be not only citizens of their various nations, but also less than whole people—anyone living in the United States when the Constitution was ratified seemed to qualify as a citizen. The only distinction was that to be elected president, a person needed to be born on American soil. (There has been some speculation that this clause was inserted specifically to keep Alexander Hamilton, who was born in Nevis in the West Indies, from the presidency.) Requirements to attain citizenship were also not discussed, but Congress was empowered to "establish a uniform rule of naturalization."

Citizenship did not mean voting. In every state, in order to qualify to vote, a person—almost always a man—needed to be twenty-one years old and either own property or pay taxes. (In New Jersey, where a technicality allowed women with property to vote, an amendment to the state constitution soon closed that loophole.) In fact, the language of both the Constitution and its first ten amendments did not explain what would later be termed "privileges and immunities" of citizenship at all. All the rights enumerated were in terms of "people," which made no distinction between citizens and noncitizens.

While the First Congress made no effort to clear up this vague concept of citizenship, it did take up how those who did not live in the United States at its founding could become "naturalized" American citizens. As John Lawrence of New York observed in the debates over naturalization in February 1790, "The reason of admitting foreigners to the rights of citizenship among us is the encouragement of emigration, as we have a large tract of country to people."

And that "large tract," mostly in the West, would need a significant influx for both the nation's economic growth and self-defense. Yet there was also general agreement that the country did not want just anybody. When discussing a residency requirement, James Madison warned, "When we are considering the advantages that may result from an easy mode of naturalization, we ought also to consider the cautions necessary to guard against abuses; it is no doubt very desirable, that we should hold out as many inducements as possible, for the worthy part of mankind to come and settle amongst us, and throw their fortunes into a common lot with ours . . . I should be exceeding sorry, sir, that our rule of naturalization excluded a single person of good fame, that really meant to incorporate himself into our society; on the other hand, I do not wish that any man should acquire the privilege, but who, in fact, is a real addition to the wealth or strength of the United States."

In the end, Madison's hesitation worked itself into the final bill. On March 26, 1790, President George Washington signed "an act to establish a uniform Rule of Naturalization" into law. It stipulated:

> That any alien, being a free white person, who shall have resided within the limits and under the jurisdiction of the United States for the term of two years, may be admitted to become a citizen thereof . . . in any one of the states wherein he shall have resided for the term of one year at least . . . that he is a person of good character, and taking the oath or affirmation prescribed by law, to support the constitution of the United States.

In addition to limiting naturalization to free whites, although just what would determine race was left unspecified, the use of "he" was not an accident. In practice, few women could become naturalized citizens, except by application with her husband, or sometimes her son. As with most matters, naturalization was left to the states to decide who qualified for United States citizenship under the law.

Although almost every member of Congress, as well as

Senator William Maclay.

President Washington, favored the limitation of "whites of good character," there were dissenting voices. Senator William Maclay of Pennsylvania wrote in his diary, "The truth of the matter is that it is a Vile bill, illiberal. Void of philanthropy and needed mending much. We Pennsylvanians act as if we believed that God made of one blood all families of the Earth."

Maclay left Congress in disgust after one term, no mending of the 1790 law to be had. In the end, the only part of the legislation that caused widespread controversy was the residency requirement, which was directly related to the understanding that over time it would become easier (for men) to vote, with the property-holding prerequisite likely to eventually disappear. Residency was raised from two years to five in 1795, and then, in 1798, with Thomas Jefferson's populists threatening to displace John Adams's more stodgy Federalists, to fourteen years. (It wouldn't help Adams, who would lose to Jefferson in 1800, not because landless whites were counted for electoral votes, but because three-fifths of the slaves were.) In 1802, with Jefferson in the President's House—it wasn't officially called the White House until 1901—the requirement was again put at five years, where it remains today.

Citizenship did not become a matter for the courts until the 1850s, and then only as an aside. The case began in 1836, when a United States Army major, Lawrence Taliaferro, performed a wedding ceremony. The groom was about forty, and the bride about ten years younger. Both were simply dressed. What made this ceremony unusual, however, was that the groom, Dred Scott, and the bride, Harriet Robinson, were both Black and, depending on whom one asked, either former or current slaves.

Dred Scott and his wife, Harriet Robinson Scott.

There was no question that both had been enslaved previously, but their owners had moved from slave states to Wisconsin, in which, according to the Missouri Compromise, slavery was outlawed. The Missouri Compromise was a law passed in 1820 that tried to maintain the balance between slave states and free states in Congress. Maine would be admitted as a free state, Missouri as a slave state, and, except for Missouri, slavery would be prohibited north of the 36°30' parallel.

Northerners insisted that meant any slave traveling from a slave state to a free state would automatically be freed. Southerners disagreed. To them, slaves were property, and it would be the same as saying if a Northerner came south with cattle, the cattle would be freed. Still, Dred and Harriet's owners must have agreed they were free, since marriages were only recognized between free people. If they were still enslaved, the ceremony would not have taken place.

The question of the Scotts' status gained importance when their owner returned to Missouri and hired the Scotts out as slaves for a local farmer. Dred Scott, backed by abolitionist lawyers, sued for his freedom in state court. He lost, as he did later in federal court. After many twists, turns, and long delays, in 1856, the case of *Dred Scott v. Sandford* finally reached the United States Supreme Court.

The chief justice in 1856 was Roger Brooke Taney (pronounced TAW-ney), a former slaveholder from Maryland who had been appointed to the high bench by another former slaveholder, President Andrew Jackson. Jackson had chosen Taney, who had been his attorney general, to favor the rights of states over those of the federal government, which included states in which slavery was an institution.

Roger B. Taney.

The Supreme Court's decision was not handed down until March 1857, with Taney writing the opinion for a 7–2 majority. During the time between when the case was argued and the decision, President James Buchanan approached some of the justices, including Taney, insisting that a definitive judgment on the legality of slavery was needed to head off the threat of war.

Taney's opinion was as definitive as Buchanan could have hoped for. He ruled not only that slaves could not be United States citizens, but also that "[a] free negro of the African race, whose ancestors were brought to this country and sold as slaves, is not a 'citizen' within the meaning of the Constitution of the United States." Since Black people—enslaved or free—could not be citizens, they had no standing to sue in federal court.

In addition, since the Fifth Amendment guaranteed the property rights of slave owners, and enslaved people were property, Congress could not pass a law that forbade slave ownership anywhere in the nation. The Missouri Compromise legislation, therefore, was unconstitutional.

Although his personal views had no bearing on the case, Taney included them anyway.

Black people, he wrote, "had for more than a century before been regarded as beings of an inferior order, and altogether unfit to associate with the white race . . . and so far inferior, that they had no rights which the white man was bound to respect."

The Dred Scott decision is, along with *Korematsu v. United States*, almost universally considered among the very worst decisions ever handed down by the Supreme Court. Roger Taney, who was otherwise a highly respected legal scholar, has been vilified, not unfairly, as epitomizing bigotry, ignorance, and intolerance. In perhaps the biggest irony of all, rather than prevent a war with his definitive judgment, Taney helped start one.

CHAPTER 2

WHITE, BLACK, . . . AND GOLD

ON JANUARY 24, 1848, a carpenter named James Marshall was supervising the construction of a sawmill for John Sutter near the American Fork River in north-central California. He noticed some metal flakes near a stream. The flakes were gold.

Marshall, Sutter, and the other workers tried to keep their find a secret, but word inevitably leaked out. By the following year, the Gold Rush had begun and upward of 80,000 would-be millionaires descended on California. San Francisco's population grew from about 800 people in 1848 to 25,000 just two years later. Most came overland or by steamship from the East, but others came from across the Pacific, almost all from China. Most Chinese people arrived intending to stay only long enough at "Gold Mountain" to allow them to return home rich. At first, the hardworking Chinese were accepted by the other miners. But as gold became scarcer and the Chinese became more plentiful—there would be 24,000 within three years—resentment developed.

Gold miners.

In 1850, California began taxing "foreign" miners. Most white immigrants avoided paying simply by saying they were American, but Chinese miners did not have the same option. Of those Chinese who did pay the tax, many became victims of violence by whites.

As a result, most Chinese gave up the hunt for gold and entered other professions. Some hired themselves out as workers in mining camps, some became farm laborers, while still others settled in cities—mostly in booming San Francisco—and either opened their own businesses or worked for white business owners. They became sought after by employers who could work them longer and harder than white workers and pay them a good deal less. For the Chinese, much like today's South and Central American immigrants, the grim working conditions and the pittance they were paid were still better than they could expect in their home country.

As the Chinese population expanded, many who had crossed the Pacific decided to remain permanently in the United States, some migrating as far east as New York. For the first time, their eligibility to apply for United States citizenship came under question, which in turn led to the question of just who was and was not "white" according to the 1790 law. Until that point, the rule of thumb for naturalization seemed to be that any immigrant who looked white and claimed to be white was allowed to apply for citizenship as white.

The issue became more complicated in 1870. In the wake of the Civil War, Congress debated whether naturalization should be altered in favor of those of "African descent." The aim was to allow any former slave or descendant of slaves to become a citizen. For the first time, whether race should be included in naturalization law at all came under question. As such, the subject of citizenship for the Chinese was also hotly contested.

The concept of extending naturalization rights to the Chinese had many supporters, almost all from the East or Midwest, where there were fewer Chinese immigrants than out west. Senator Charles Sumner of Massachusetts said, "I content myself for the present with saying that the word 'white' be struck from the statute book." Pennsylvania Senator Simon Cameron agreed.

"I am in favor of the position of the Senator from Massachusetts because it invites into our country everybody: the negro, the Irishman, the German, the Frenchman, the Scotchman, the Englishman, and the Chinaman. I will welcome every man." Richard Yates and Lyman Trumbull, both of Illinois, supported multiracial citizenship, as did Indiana's Oliver Morton.

Not everyone was so open-minded. Opposition to Chinese citizenship was almost universal in the West, much of it expressed in openly racist terms. Representative James Johnson of California, who had earlier introduced a resolution stating that the Fifteenth Amendment "never intended that Chinese or Mongolians should become voters," told his colleagues, "I hope a large majority of the good people of this country believe its future greatness can best be secured by preserving the Caucasian blood in its purity; that the white is superior to the Chinaman; that our country would be better off peopled entirely with our own kind than if mixed with an inferior and degraded race."

He added later, "How can any lover of this country ask for free Chinese immigration, which is Chinese citizenship and Chinese suffrage? . . . If the Hottentot, the cannibal from the jungles of Africa, the West India negro, the wild Indian, and the Chinaman are to become a ruling element in this country, then call your ministers from abroad, bring your missionaries home, tear down your school houses, convert your churches into dens and brothels, wherein our young may receive fatal lessons to end in rotting bones, decaying and putrid flesh, poisoned blood, leprous bodies, and leprous souls."

With western congressmen immovable in opposition, the 1870 law simply read, "The naturalization laws are hereby extended to aliens of African nativity and to persons of African descent." Whether intended or not, this phrasing also opened the citizenship door to those who had never been slaves at all, and, for the first time in American history, people who were not "white" were officially allowed to become citizens of the United States. The law did not, however, help in creating a legal definition of "white."

By the 1870s, Chinese immigration continued to increase, and white communities in the West grew more and more determined to halt what they saw as pollution by an inferior race. Chinese laborers were key targets, since they were lowering wages for white workers. Early union leaders, such as Denis Kearney of the Workingmen's Party of California and Daniel Cronin of the Washington Territory's Knights of Labor, petitioned West Coast politicians to stanch the flow of Chinese labor. California responded by enacting a series of laws aimed at denying Chinese immigrants, none of whom were citizens, either employment or housing. For example, an 1870 San Francisco ordinance called the "Sanitary Act" said that all housing must have five hundred cubic feet of air for each occupant. The law was enforced only in Chinatown, where immigrants, most of whom were working for impossibly low wages, lived in horribly cramped conditions. Many Chinese

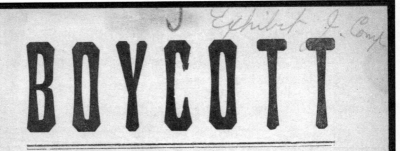

BOYCOTT

A General Boycott has been declared upon all **CHINESE** and **JAPANESE** Restaurants, Tailor Shops and Wash Houses. Also all persons employing them in any capacity.

All Friends and Sympathizers of Organized Labor will assist us in this fight against the lowering Asiatic standards of living and of morals.

AMERICA vs. ASIA
Progress vs. Retrogression

Are the considerations involved.

BY ORDER OF

Silver Bow Trades and Labor Assembly and Butte Miners' Union

An anti-Chinese and -Japanese poster issued by labor unions.

people who could not pay the steep fines were sent to equally overcrowded local jails.

Although few Chinese immigrants could speak English, they acquired a sophisticated understanding of the American legal system. Each time California passed a discriminatory law, Chinese businessmen hired white lawyers to bring suit in either state or federal court. To the consternation of the authorities, the lawsuits were often successful.

Another focus was Chinese women, who were widely assumed to be prostitutes. It seemed clear that only action by the federal government could stem Chinese immigration. In 1875, Horace Page, a California Republican, sponsored a bill to "end the danger of cheap Chinese labor and immoral Chinese women."

Page was born in New York in 1833, but moved to Placerville, California, when he was twenty. He started a successful sawmill business, then a livery stable, and then made a series of astute business investments, becoming a respected member of his community. He was vocal about curbing the power of the railroads and requiring them to pay higher fees and taxes, both statewide and locally. Although he claimed no interest in politics, he was persuaded to run for Congress in 1872 and won an upset victory in a campaign marked by a good deal of mudslinging on both sides.

During his first term, Page attacked the exorbitant prices charged by private firms that carried the United States mail and succeeded in saving the government an estimated

Horace Page, California
representative, 1873–1883.

$3 million. But Page's targets were not only railroads and government price-gougers. "Ever mindful of the Asiatic curse resting upon California, at the first opportunity and within a few weeks after his arrival in Washington," Page introduced a resolution demanding that the United States "check or altogether prevent Chinese immigration to the United States."

Page also discovered that when the naturalization laws were transcribed into the Revised Statutes—the first official record of the laws of the United States printed by the government—the requirement that an immigrant be "white" had been left out. He brought it to the attention of Congress and "free white persons" was reaffirmed in February 1875.

The law Horace Page proposed would be the first in American history that restricted the entry of specific "undesirable" elements. Rather than target the Chinese as a race—which would have run afoul of a treaty signed in 1868—Page proposed banning "coolies," unskilled Chinese laborers, and Chinese women entering the country with the intention of becoming prostitutes or "concubines." Since Chinese marriage ceremonies were not recognized as legal, this meant just about every Chinese woman arriving at an American port. As Page put it in his speech in Congress, he intended to "place a dividing line between vice and virtue," and "send the brazen harlot who openly flaunts her wickedness in the faces of our wives and daughters back to her native country." White Americans, he added, were "stout-hearted people" who, "with their wives and children . . . staked everything" to come to California but now faced a "deadly blight."

Page had a good deal of support from labor groups, churches, and other politicians who viewed the Chinese as a winning campaign issue. But he also had the backing from some unexpected sources, such as the American Medical Association, which announced that the Chinese, especially the women, were carriers of diseases that would resist cures if they infected whites.

In the end, Page's bill had little trouble in Congress, easily passing in both houses. It was signed into law by President Ulysses Grant on March 3, 1875, two days after the president had signed the Civil Rights Act of 1875, guaranteeing Black Americans equal access to theaters, restaurants, public conveyances, and hotels. (Eight years later, the Supreme Court would declare that law unconstitutional. The Page Act, however, would stand.)

While the law was only marginally successfully at keeping out men from China—western employers were not displeased with laborers whom they could work to exhaustion and pay almost nothing—the Page Act virtually eliminated the entry of Chinese women.

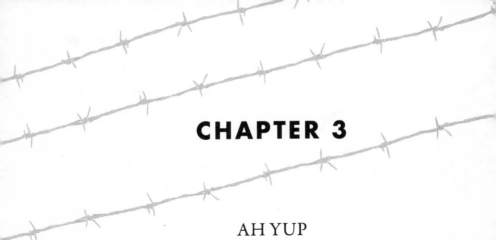

CHAPTER 3

AH YUP

THE 1870 LAW HAD contained no specific mention of the Chinese, and so, even with the Page Act in place, the status of Chinese immigrants already in the United States was not clear. The United States lacked a national bureau of immigration, so judges in individual states—not even necessarily federal judges—were left to decide whether or not Chinese people were to be considered "white" for purposes of naturalization. Away from the West Coast, where anti-Chinese sentiment was highest, this question did not arouse much controversy,

In 1878, for example, the *New York Herald* reported, "For the first time in the history of the city of New York native born live Chinaman has been admitted to all the privileges of citizenship provided by the Constitution of the United States . . . The question of the naturalization of Mongolians has been a mooted one for many years, and the constantly increasing emigration of that mysterious and thrifty race has intensified the popular interest in the settlement of this difficult problem."

The new citizen, Wong Ah Yee, who was granted citizenship by a New York State judge, was described as "of unusual intelligence and ability . . . married to an Irishwoman and doing a good cigar-making business in Baxter street."

In the West, however, "unusual intelligence and ability" would be of little importance to anti-Asian white people. Even the relative trickle of new immigrants from China who could circumvent the Page Act was too much for what these whites came to speak of as a "plague." State and city officials demanded that Congress and the president take steps to prevent the West Coast, and eventually all of America, from being overrun. Once more, among the most vocal advocates of ending Chinese immigration were the leaders of America's growing labor movement, who saw low-cost Chinese labor as fatal to their own efforts to improve the wages of union members.

In addition, California and the other western states had stepped up their efforts to strangle Chinese immigrants already in country. States and cities enacted laws aimed at denying Chinese immigrants either employment or housing, and they were also subject to beatings, theft of their property, and denial of almost all government protection. The small segment of the Chinese population that had become successful realized that unless they could become citizens, they could do nothing to fight discrimination. One Chinese leader noted, "The moment you appear at the ballot box, you are a man and

Lorenzo Sawyer.

a brother and are treated to cigars, whiskeys and beers."

But without citizenship, there would be no voting, and so, in 1878, they sponsored a test case in which a Chinese immigrant named Ah Yup applied for naturalization because, they asserted, "Mongolians," as all East Asians were classified, should be seen as "white." The case was heard in federal circuit presided over by Judge Lorenzo Sawyer.

Unlike many Californians, Sawyer had not expressed any adverse sentiments toward the Chinese, although he was a close associate of Leland Stanford, a former governor of California and soon-to-be founder of a university, who had done so often. (To say nothing of the fact that thousands of Chinese workers had died building the transcontinental railroad that made Stanford an immense fortune.) In addition, Sawyer was a thorough and respected legal scholar, appointed to the federal bench by Ulysses Grant after a stint as chief justice of the California courts.

Sawyer was aware that he was the first judge to be asked to

create a legal definition of "white," and he undertook a careful, meticulous analysis, considering not only the evidence presented by the opposing lawyers but also examining scientific definitions of race. For the science, Sawyer relied mainly on the work of Johann Blumenbach, a German anthropologist and race theorist. While much of Blumenbach's work laid the groundwork for modern anthropology, some of his other theories turned out to be self-serving claptrap. He used skull size and shape to separate humans into five distinct racial groups: Caucasian, Ethiopian, American Indian, Mongolian, and Malay. Predictably, he found "whites" as the most advanced and called them "Caucasian," because he believed they had descended from Adam and Eve and originated on the southern slopes of Mount Caucasus in the country of Georgia. All the other races represented a "degeneration" from the Caucasian ideal.

Words, Sawyer wrote, should be taken in the ordinary sense, and "white" didn't refer simply to skin tone. "Those called white may be found in every shade from the lightest blonde to the most swarthy brunette," yet "as ordinarily used everywhere in the United States, one would scarcely fail to understand that the party employing the words 'white person' would intend a person of the Caucasian race." Thus, according to Blumenbach, as well as other race theorists, the Chinese, as Mongolians, were not "white."

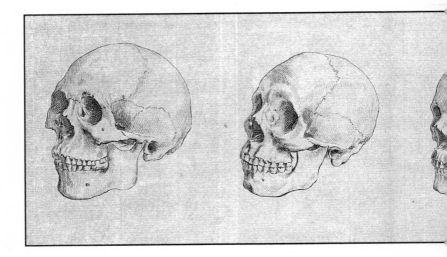

Sawyer also relied on the congressional debates leading up to the 1870 naturalization law, in which those who opposed Charles Sumner's motion to remove the word "white" from the statute often did so specifically to ensure banning the Chinese. In his conclusion, he wrote, "A Mongolian is not a 'white person' within the meaning of the term as used in the naturalization laws of the United States." As a result, no Chinese immigrant could apply for American citizenship regardless of how long they had lived in the United States.

But Horace Page was not finished. "There has hardly been a session of Congress since his election, that he has not introduced an anti-Chinese resolution or bill . . . restrictive legislation on Chinese immigration . . . was ever present on his mind." On April 12, 1882, Page introduced a bill

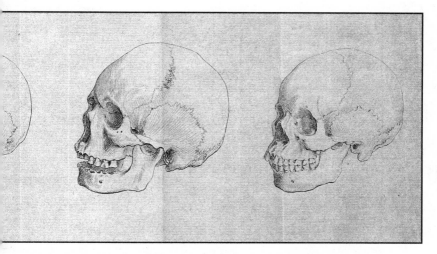

"Blumenbach's five skulls—Mongolian, American, Caucasian, Malayan and Ethiopian races—from the treatise 'De generis humani varietate nativa.'"

in the House of Representatives that would effectively ban all Chinese immigrants from entering the United States. Although specifically aimed at laborers, the bill was drafted in such a way as to make it extraordinarily difficult for anyone Chinese to prove he was *not* a laborer. The bill also reaffirmed that the Chinese already in the country could not become citizens.

Page's bill sailed through both houses of Congress and was signed by President Chester A. Arthur on May 6, 1882. It was the first immigration law passed in the United States that barred a specific national or ethnic group. Coupled with the Page Act, the Chinese Exclusion Act halted virtually all Chinese immigration for almost a century.

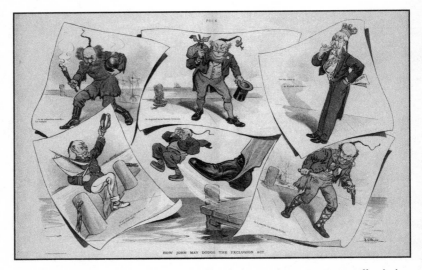

This racist 1905 cartoon shows Uncle Sam's boot kicking a Chinese immigrant off a dock as part of an anti-Chinese immigration campaign. Other vignettes show how the Chinese could possibly immigrate to the United States.

Although most in the West were pleased, many employers rued the loss of a labor pool that could be pushed to superhuman limits for subhuman pay. They immediately sought a replacement and soon found one.

CHAPTER 4

ENTER THE JAPANESE

IN JULY 1853, COMMODORE Matthew Perry led a flotilla of four warships into Edo Harbor (now Tokyo), with instructions to either persuade or compel the reclusive Japanese to open trade with the West. Since previous overtures had been rebuffed, Perry arrived with permission to use force to gain compliance. Though at first the Japanese refused to send anyone of significant rank to speak with the invader, Perry's ships were equipped with a formidable array of modern cannons and eventually they relented. After a second visit the following year, Perry succeeded in "opening" Japan to Western trade and influence.

As more Americans and Europeans arrived, the Japanese became aware that isolation had also resulted in diminished technological progress. In 1868, a group of nobles bent on reform and modernization overthrew the Tokugawa shogunate, which had ruled Japan for two centuries, and established a new government under fifteen-year-old Matsuhito, who was

A Japanese painting of one of Commodore Perry's "Black Ships" in Tokyo Bay, July 8, 1853.

dubbed Emperor Meiji ("Enlightened"). The new rulers of what would be called the "Meiji Restoration" immediately took to breaking down the old order, sweeping away the caste system, a feudal economy, a medieval military, restrictive education, and, mostly, the unwillingness to interact with other nations.

Later that year, under an agreement between the Meiji government and King Kalakaua of Hawai'i, a group of contract laborers left Japan to work on the Hawaiian* sugar

---

* The proper punctuation between the final two letters of "Hawaii" is an okina, which appears as an inverted upside-down apostrophe, but the official spelling was changed to eliminate it when Hawaii became a state in 1959. "Hawaiian" was never punctuated. This book will use the post-1959 spelling.

皇室御尊影

Emperor Meiji and his family.

plantations. Called "gannenmono," for "first year," the group consisted of 143 men—most in their twenties—6 women, and 1 child. Brokered by an American merchant, Eugene Van Reed, who had been appointed to serve as the Kingdom of Hawaii's consul in Japan, the workers would be paid four dollars for twenty-six days of work per month and also receive room, board, and medical care. The contract was for five years, with almost all of the men assigned to work in the sugarcane fields.

In the short term, the experiment seemed a failure. Japanese workers did not fare well cutting sugarcane in the intense heat, and within two years more than a third had returned home. Another third chose to sail in the other direction and settle

Japanese workers cutting sugarcane in the 1930s.

in the United States, most in California. The rest remained in Hawaii, married local women, and began families. Those fifty became the roots of what turned into a thriving Japanese community, a vibrant segment of Hawaiian society, which experienced little of the bigotry that the Chinese were subject to on the mainland.

But for Japan, exporting a few laborers was only the beginning. As one scholar wrote, "Over the next twenty years [from 1868] Japan experienced a complete overhaul of its political and social structures and embraced Westernization, taking the world by surprise with the breakneck speed of its modernization." As part of that overhaul, Japan exported its culture first to Europe and then to the United States. Japanese art and design became all the rage, with the French coining the term "japonais" to describe a school of art that borrowed liberally from painting, scrolls, pottery, and other artifacts that were sent west by the Meiji government. Artists such as James Abbott McNeill Whistler and Vincent van Gogh would be deeply influenced by Japanese craftsmen, and Gilbert and Sullivan's *The Mikado* would be an enormous success, first in Britain and then in the United States.

It was not until 1876, however, that Japanese culture exploded onto the American stage. At the grand American centennial exposition in Philadelphia, America's first world's fair, the Japanese exhibition proved to be one of the event's most popular attractions. (And the competition was intense.

Among the other marvels were the bicycle, the gasoline engine, a giant locomotive, the telephone, the typewriter, root beer, bananas, and Heinz ketchup.) Two years later, when former president Ulysses Grant stopped for an extended stay in Japan on his around-the-world tour, America's fascination

Japanese exhibition at the 1876 Centennial.

grew all the more. He wrote, "My visit to Japan has been the most pleasant of all my travels. The country is beautifully cultivated, the scenery is grand, and the people, from the highest to the lowest, the most kindly and the most clean in the world. My reception and entertainment has been the most extravagant I have ever known, or even read of."

A painting showing a reception for Ulysses Grant and his wife in Ueno, Japan, given by the Meiji emperor and empress.

All this was soon translated into commerce. "The American interest in Japan created a booming export market, especially for art and artifacts from Japan's feudal past, of which the new western-focused government was eager to rid itself. Japanese fashions, performing arts, and philosophy began to enjoy popularity in America. Kimonos, paper parasols, and folding fans became fashionable among ladies of all social ranks."

Although this exalted view of Japanese culture was largely confined to the eastern United States, a sprinkling of well-educated students and entrepreneurs began to migrate to West Coast cities, all of which led to a tentative belief that the Japanese were somehow "superior" to the Chinese, both personally and culturally. And so, after the Chinese Exclusion Act eliminated the source of cheap labor that western farmers, timber barons, and industrialists had come to rely on, Japan seemed the perfect replacement.

Between 1885 and 1895, 30,000 Japanese contract workers sailed east, most settling in Hawaii, but 2,000 continuing on to California. A treaty signed in 1894 guaranteed the right of immigration to the United States to citizens of Japan. At first, these new workers were welcomed by employers who congratulated themselves on solving their labor problem with a people they saw as clean and morally upright. More Japanese people came until, in 1900, more than 12,000 arrived in a single year. Still, there were fewer than 25,000 in the entire United States.

As their numbers increased, however, the presence of so many Asians—none of whom could apply for citizenship—began to evoke the same white backlash that had befallen the Chinese. Suddenly, the Japanese became "sneaky," "clannish," "out to undermine white society," with Japanese women denounced as prostitutes. The artifacts of Japanese culture that had so fascinated white society ten and twenty years before became symbols of a foreign race that could never blend into American society.

But the West was growing, and the demand for low-paid agricultural workers was growing right along with it. Most Japanese immigrants became West Coast farm laborers, while others worked in lumber or mining, or started small businesses, such as general stores. White farmers and growers were pleased to have a replacement workforce that could be pushed to exhaustion seven days per week for next to no money—jobs few whites wanted anyway.

Organized labor, which had initially been accepting of the new immigrants, began to accuse Japanese workers of destroying the lives of American workers, many of whom were immigrants from Europe. In its official magazine, the American Federation of Labor declared, "White workers, including ignorant ones and the newcomers from southern and eastern Europe, possessed qualities enabling them to join and contribute to the labor movement. They could be taught the fundamentals of unionism and would stand shoulder to shoulder with faithful workers . . . Unable to be 'assimilated,' the Japanese could not become 'union men.'"

Many ordinary white citizens took that view one step further and insisted the Japanese could never become American at all.

CHAPTER 5

BIRTHRIGHT

ALTHOUGH CHINESE IMMIGRATION HAD been banned and the Chinese people already in the United States could not become citizens, one key question remained: Were children born in the United States to Chinese immigrant parents American citizens?

The answer seemed to be yes, since Section 1 of the Fourteenth Amendment stated, "All persons born or naturalized in the United States, and subject to the jurisdiction thereof, are citizens of the United States and of the state wherein they reside." While the amendment had clearly been intended to guarantee citizenship to freed slaves, there was nothing in the amendment that limited its application, unless "subject to the jurisdiction thereof" could somehow be turned into a restriction.

There were two theories that could apply. The first was called "jus soli" or "law of the soil." It meant that citizenship was determined by where a person was born. The second was "jus sanguinis" or "law of the blood," which meant that citizenship was determined by the nationality or ethnicity of one's parents. Although the United States had always been a "jus soli" nation, there was no law that said it had to remain that way.

When the Fourteenth Amendment was adopted in 1868, there were so few Chinese people in the United States that questions of their birthright citizenship had not come up. Even by 1880, there were barely one thousand American-born Chinese children in the entire nation.

The following year, that number was increased by one when a boy named Wong Kim Ark was born in San Francisco. His parents had lived in California for more than a decade but could not apply for American citizenship. But what about their child?

Wong's parents returned to China when he was in his late teens. He visited them in 1890 and returned to the United States some months later without incident. Four years later, he traveled to China once more, again remaining for some months before returning to the United States in August 1895.

This time, Wong Kim Ark was denied entry by a customs inspector in San Francisco. Even though he had documents to prove that he had been born in the United States, the inspector claimed he was not a citizen.

Identification photograph on affidavit "In the Matter of Wong Kim Ark, Native Born Citizen of the United States."

Wong was held offshore for five months in a ship anchored in San Francisco Bay. In November, he was approached by representatives of a group called the Six Companies and asked to start a lawsuit challenging his exclusion. The Six Companies, also known as the Chinese Consolidated Benevolent Association, was a powerful organization comprised of the six most important huiguan—district associations—in San Francisco. The group focused most of its efforts on the basic needs of Chinese immigrants, such as communicating with relatives in China, medical care, or arranging for the dead to be shipped across the Pacific for burial. They also, however, mounted a series of legal challenges to anti-Chinese city ordinances and state laws, many of which, to the consternation of white supremacists, were successful.

Preventing birthright citizenship from being denied was crucial. Even as children, birthright citizens could conceivably have property registered in their names and enter into contracts, both of which state and local authorities had restricted for noncitizens with discriminatory legislation.

What whites feared most was that birthright citizens had the right to vote. "If this young Chinaman should be declared to be a citizen," one newspaper complained, "then there are several thousand Chinese citizens in this State, and of course they will be entitled to the ballot . . . It is enough to make one shudder to contemplate."

The Six Companies always used white lawyers (Chinese

people were prohibited from being lawyers), and for Wong, they hired prominent Democrat Thomas Riordan. He filed a motion on Wong's behalf that was argued in federal district court in San Francisco in January 1896. The government "claimed that a Chinese could not become a citizen of this country, even though born here, under the Fourteenth Amendment to the Constitution." Since Wong was born to

Officers of the Chinese Six Companies.

parents who were subjects of China, the United States attorney insisted, he was a subject of China and not, in the words of the Fourteenth Amendment, "subject to the jurisdiction" of the United States. In fact, children born to Chinese nationals were Chinese citizens as well if their birth was registered in China, as Wong Kim Ark's was.

Riordan simply said that no matter how much the government tried to dodge the issue, the United States was a jus soli nation, had always been so, and the Fourteenth Amendment had been enacted under that rule. Like it or not, Wong Kim Ark was a citizen of the United States, entitled to all the privileges and immunities that citizenship transmitted. And the case went beyond the Chinese. If Wong's birthright were denied, anyone born in the United States whose parents were immigrants would lose their citizenship as well.

On January 3, 1896, the district court judge ruled that "Chinese born in this country . . . are citizens of the United States, and may exercise the elective franchise, and may go and come whenever and wherever they please." The judge had scarcely pounded his gavel to end the proceedings when the government announced its intention to appeal to the Supreme Court. But the justices were in no hurry and would not hear oral arguments until March 1897. While the case was pending, officials throughout California made every effort to prevent native-born Chinese Americans from voting, which the Chinese were equally determined to do. "They will be, at least and by all means, examined most severely on the educational qualification, and to this end the 'native sons' are now learning the constitution by heart."

The issue was put to rest on March 29, 1898, when, in a 6–2 decision, the Supreme Court ruled for Wong. Justice Horace Gray wrote the opinion. He narrowed the question to a child "born in the United States, of parents of Chinese descent, who, at the time of his birth, are subjects of the Emperor of China, but have a permanent domicile and residence in the United States, and are there carrying on business." But the Fourteenth Amendment made no mention of the parents having "permanent domicile," so Gray limited the reach of the decision to a certain category of immigrant.

From there Gray went on at great length to cite examples in English common law, as well as other cases in American jurisprudence, concluding that none were "inconsistent with the ancient rule of citizenship by birth within the dominion." The Fourteenth Amendment also fell under this umbrella, so Wong Kim Ark's American citizenship was affirmed.

Gray's opinion was an unpleasant surprise for West Coast white supremacists. After all, just two years earlier, the same roster of justices had ignored Fourteenth Amendment guarantees in *Plessy v. Ferguson* and upheld a blatantly racist Louisiana law forcing Black American citizens to ride in smoky, dirty, substandard railroad cars on the grounds that separate facilities were constitutionally acceptable as long as they were "equal."

But perhaps the real reason for the Court's seeming pivot away from the shameless racism of *Plessy* can be found buried in the middle of Justice Gray's opinion. "To hold that the Fourteenth Amendment of the Constitution excludes from citizenship the children, born in the United States, of citizens or subjects of other countries would be to deny citizenship to thousands of persons of English, Scotch, Irish, German, or other European parentage who have always been considered and treated as citizens of the United States."

The image held by western whites of the Chinese arriving by the thousands to overrun white civilization had not persuaded the justices, almost all of whom were from the east. There were so few native-born Americans of Chinese descent that they were less concerned with them than the much larger number of native-born children from "desirable" northern European countries.

Although *United States v. Wong Kim Ark* has remained a powerful precedent for more than a century, a group of conservative justices, led by Clarence Thomas, have suggested that the question of birthright citizenship be revisited, especially in the case of children born in the United States to immigrants who are in violation of current naturalization law. Millions of adults and children who have always considered themselves American might then be left without citizenship not only in the United States, but also in the country their parents left.

CHAPTER 6

EXCLUSION

ALTHOUGH THE DECISION IN *Wong Kim Ark* protected a tiny minority of Chinese people in America, it also inflamed anti-Asian sentiment, especially in the West. Politicians of both parties seized on race hatred as a reliable campaign issue and

James Duval Phelan.

competed with each other in bigotry. For the next three decades, one of the most successful of these was also one of the most cultured men in California.

James Duval Phelan was a highly educated heir to a banking and real estate fortune before becoming a banker himself and a fixture in San Francisco society. He gave elegant dinners at the exclusive Bohemian Club and was famed for his exquisite taste. A friend wrote that Phelan "financed California playwrights, artists, and sculptors and their creations, together with European art and sculpture, filled his house and gardens. He would have preferred being a great poet rather than a millionaire . . . In the outdoor theater, back of the patio and swimming pool, his most enjoyable afternoons were experienced when poets read aloud their original verse. He, himself, contributed excellent sonnets."

In 1896, he resigned as president of the San Francisco Art

Society gathering at Phelan's Villa Montalvo.

Association to run for mayor, vowing "to rid the city of the domination of bosses." Although he had no experience in politics, Phelan won easily and came into office promising to improve the city's water supply, to work to pass a revised city charter, to cut "the waste and extravagance which is the cause of high taxation," and to ensure that "municipal offices are conducted without extravagance, favoritism, waste or corruption."

Although when he first took office in January 1897, Phelan seemed no more anti-Asian than most members of the city's aristocracy, he soon realized that preaching Chinese and Japanese exclusion was a key to continued popularity. Phelan then became the city's most reliable spokesman for white supremacy and gained the enthusiastic support of San Francisco's increasingly powerful labor unions, as well as anti-Asian business leaders, such as newspaper magnates William Randolph Hearst and V. S. McClatchy.

Exclusion advocates got a boost in February 1900, when dead rats were found on the streets of Chinatown. The following month saw the death of a number of Chinatown residents. City medical officials, after copious testing, determined the cause to be bubonic plague. Although, through increased awareness and proper sanitation, the disease would no longer spread unabated and kill thousands, just the presence of what had been called the "Black Death" spread panic across the city.

On March 7, Mayor Phelan, who missed no opportunity to call the Chinese and the Japanese filthy races and menaces to public health, ordered Chinatown and the two tiny Japantowns to be roped off and quarantined. No other neighborhood in the city received similar treatment.

Ordinarily, Phelan would have been cheered on all sides, but the prospect of plague in the West's largest city promised to strangle shipping and commerce. California governor Henry Gage, fearing economic disaster, issued a string of denials, claiming the reports of plague were politically motivated.

Two men dissecting rats nailed to shingles, San Francisco, California.

San Francisco newspapers supported him. One ran an article the day after the quarantine called "Fake Plague Part of Plot to Plunder." It opened, "There is not bubonic plague in San Francisco," and went on to accuse those who put forth such a notion of making "a bold attempt to blackmail the city out of funds to feed a horde of hungry office-seekers who compose Mayor Phelan's only following." Phelan must have been stunned at being attacked for singling out Asians as carriers of a dreaded disease.

The doctors and Phelan would be proven correct, however, and San Francisco would deal with the plague outbreak, indeed centered in Chinatown, for more than three years. The quarantine would turn out to have been exactly the proper course, and it helped limit deaths from the disease to just over one hundred. Nonetheless, because most public officials and every newspaper described the situation as a hoax, Chinese and especially Japanese community leaders were convinced this was merely another attempt to cast them as scapegoats for the city's ills and provide an excuse to isolate them rather than the disease.

There was a good deal of evidence to support their conclusions. On May 7, 1900, an "enthusiastic and largely attended mass meeting . . . under the direction of the united labor organizations of this city" met "to protest the violations of the Chinese exclusion act and the alarming influx of Japanese laborers."

Although Mayor Phelan was one of the featured speakers, perhaps the meeting's most important speaker was Edward A. Ross, a Stanford sociology professor. Ross told the crowd, "The Chinese and Japanese were impossible among us because they cannot assimilate with us; they represent a different and an inferior civilization to our own and mean by their presence the degradation of American labor and American life." Ross thundered, "It would be better for us if we were to turn our guns upon every vessel bringing Japanese to our shores rather than to permit them to land."

At the end of the meeting, the Labor Council drafted resolutions calling for a new and stronger Chinese Exclusion Act, and "the adoption of an act of Congress or the adoption of such other measures as may be necessary for the total exclusion of all classes of Japanese." One of their justifications was "the assumed virtue of the Japanese, i.e., *their partial adoption of American customs, makes them the more dangerous as competitors.*" The Japanese, then, were to be excluded both because they were unwilling to assimilate with Americans and because they were successful at doing very same thing.

Japanese community leaders in San Francisco realized they needed an organization similar to the Six Companies. But unlike the Six Companies, which aimed at protecting the legal rights of ordinary Chinese people without integration into white society, the Japanese Association of America sought to convince whites of their desire to become "true Americans."

It was "devoted to raising all of the standards of the Japanese in this country and of genuinely aiding Americanization . . . taking the lead in all movements designed to promote a better understanding between the Americans and the Japanese here, and to inculcate in the hearts and minds of the latter a devotion to and an understanding of the spirit of America."

But the spirit of America, at least on the West Coast, did not include whites welcoming those whose skin color and facial features did not match their own. Led by James Phelan, they pressured Congress for exclusion legislation. The Japanese government, hoping to keep America as an ally while it built up its military, agreed, in July 1900, to issue no additional passports to Japanese menial laborers intending to sail for the United States. With that victory, Phelan seemed on the road to higher office, but workers turned out to have more on their minds than Asian immigration.

CHAPTER 7

THE WORKERS ...

LABOR UNREST IN SAN Francisco had been simmering for years. Union members wanted shorter hours and higher wages, but employers refused to give in.

In September 1900, McNab & Smith, one of the city's largest hauling firms, fired members of a newly formed union of teamsters and refused to hire them back unless they quit the group. Michael Casey, the head of the union, which had only a few dozen members, called on all of McNab & Smith's drivers to walk out. Teamsters worked long hours, sometimes seven days a week, for low pay, and so almost one hundred drivers supported the union men. The company hired all the workers back the same day.

Word got around and within weeks, more than one thousand drivers had joined Casey's union. Casey then threatened a full-blown strike if the members did not get a raise in pay and better working conditions. The owners reluctantly agreed to a standard contract across the industry—a twelve-hour day,

Local 85 at a social gathering, 1905.

with overtime afterward or on Sunday, and a substantial pay increase.

Sensing weakness among the owners, members of fourteen waterfront unions—fifteen thousand men—joined together to establish the City Front Federation. If they went on strike, the waterfront would be completely shut down.

The owners refused to give in. An "Employers' Association" was formed in secret to "check the growing evils . . . of strikes and boycotts." Although details of its activities and even its existence were kept from the public, by summer 1901, as many

San Francisco waterfront workers, 1901.

as three hundred businesses had joined, each pledging $1,000 to blunt the union threat. With two powerful groups facing off, conflict was inevitable, and the teamsters were once again the spark.

On July 20, union teamsters refused to handle the baggage

of a group that hired an anti-union hauler that had refused to be a party to the standard contract. The hauler, with support from the Employers' Association, fired the union members who refused to unload the cargo—which were all of them— and hired replacement workers to do the job. Other owners followed suit, and one thousand union members were fired within days.

Mayor Phelan was forced to pick a side. The unions liked him for his anti-Asian stance, but members of the Employers' Association were his friends and business associates, men with whom his relationships went back decades. He chose his friends. Phelan ordered the police to accompany the replacement drivers and protect them against anyone who attempted to impede deliveries.

At first, the teamsters chose nonconfrontation and confined their activities to peaceful protest, but violence seemed inevitable. It began on July 25, when police attacked a picket line. A police captain ordered his men to charge the crowd with clubs, and half a dozen union men were badly beaten.

The following night, a patrolman found himself surrounded by an angry crowd of strikers. Other police showed up and charged the strikers with clubs. The crowd kept increasing until there were more than one thousand people on the street. The police and the strikers fought one another with clubs and rocks, until eventually both sides withdrew.

Employers' Association members issued an ultimatum to

the workers to quit their unions or be fired. The city's workers' groups responded by calling a general strike. The president of the Labor Council announced, "We have things just where we want them." The next day, the port was shut down. "Vessels were deserted by their sailors and firemen and could neither take on nor discharge cargoes. There was no activity about the wharfs; the street traffic was again almost entirely suspended."

Once more, the strikers offered to negotiate for higher wages and shorter hours. But the Employers' Association stood firm, confident that the workers could not afford to remain on strike without any money coming in. In response, the workers grew more militant and, by August, there was widespread violence, wholesale arrests, and even some deaths.

Phelan was again forced to choose, and again, after a failed attempt to mediate, he chose the employers. The police assigned to guard the replacement workers were increased, many pulled from their regular duties patrolling the city streets. Skirmishes between police and strikers became more common. Phelan was denounced as a traitor to the labor movement and there seemed little chance that he could be reelected that November.

With Phelan an unacceptable candidate, and the strike threatened with collapse if members could not feed their families, a small group of union leaders met to try to win their war with the owners at the ballot box. They began to formulate plans to run pro-labor candidates in the November election.

A scab, or strikebreaker, teamster with police escort, 1901.

Although a number of unions joined up, the Union Labor Party, as it called itself, remained rudderless. They announced a convention in September to draw up an official platform and nominate candidates, but the Employers' Association, and almost everyone else, treated the new party as something of a joke with no chance to outpoll either of the major parties.

Almost everyone. There was a man who took it very seriously; he would go on to become one of the oddest and most unique political bosses in American history.

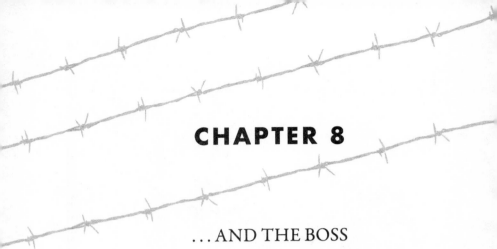

CHAPTER 8

...AND THE BOSS

ABRAHAM RUEFF WAS BORN in San Francisco in 1864. His father was a successful Jewish merchant whose wealth allowed his family to avoid at least overt anti-Semitism. Young Abe was a prodigy. He would eventually speak eight languages, including Cantonese; graduate from the University of California, Berkeley, at eighteen with high honors; breeze through law school; and join the California bar at the minimum age of twenty-one.

Ruef (he dropped the second "f") entered politics committed to good government. For a time, he traded ideas in a correspondence with another young reformer in New York, Theodore Roosevelt. But San Francisco was a poor place to be an idealist. It was run by a political machine that controlled both parties and regularly used graft and strong-arm tactics to ensure continued control. Ruef eventually decided that if he could not improve the political culture, he would dominate it.

Abe Ruef, the "Curly Boss," 1907.

When he heard of the Union Labor Party's convention, Abe Ruef decided to attend.

Almost immediately, using brains, political savvy, and charm, Ruef took over. He authored a declaration of policy for the group that was "designed to gain the support of workingmen without alienating others." A major item, as it must be with every attempt to woo union members, was a strict program of Asian exclusion. To head the ticket and run for mayor, Ruef chose a tall, good-looking, affable family man,

Eugene E. Schmitz.

Eugene Schmitz, a violinist, orchestra leader, and head of the musicians' union. Schmitz had not a shred of political experience and up to that point had no intention of acquiring any.

But with Ruef urging and flattering him along, Schmitz proved to be an excellent student. He memorized both the California constitution and the San Francisco city articles, and then, at Ruef's elbow, was introduced to dozens of the most important people in the business and political communities. Schmitz was a natural orator and, since Ruef also wrote his speeches, had just the right things to say. Still, as the election neared, few gave "Handsome Gene" much chance to be San Francisco's next mayor.

On the streets, the strikers were growing desperate. The City Front Federation insisted they would stay out as long as it took, but some of the strikers, out of money, had begun to drift back to work. Frustration boiled over on the night of September 28, 1901, when police and strikers engaged in a bloody brawl. Newspapers used the incident to turn the public against the unions. "Kearny Street between Market and Post streets bore every evidence yesterday of the terrible battle fought in the early hours of the morning between a horde of crazed strikers . . . and a brave band of five men fighting for their lives. Windows shattered, signs indented, awnings ripped, and buildings furrowed with bullets were the mute evidences of the latest riot that darkens the pages of the history of San

Francisco." The Employers' Association donated $200,000 to the police to increase manpower and the city braced for war.

But the Kearny Street battle was the strikers' last gasp. On October 2, a settlement was announced in which the Employers' Association conceded nothing that they had not been willing to give up in July. But in a larger sense, the strike would be a turning point in big city politics.

Phelan, as expected, did not run for reelection. Instead, the Democrats nominated a bland Phelan acolyte, Joseph Tobin, while the Republicans Party ran the equally lackluster city auditor, Asa Wells. For workers, there was little to choose between them. Bitter and defeated as they were, a new political party dedicated to workers' rights began to seem attractive and Abe Ruef was just the man to mobilize the disaffected, while persuading traditional party supporters at the same time that a third-party candidacy was just what San Francisco needed to finally put an end to rampant corruption.

When the results were reported, Schmitz had received 21,896 votes, Wells 17,696, and Tobin only 12,644. The *San Francisco Call* reported, "People Rebuke Bosses." Schmitz himself said, "I regard my election as a just and overwhelming rebuke to bossism." In fact, San Francisco had elected a tool of the most corrupt boss of all, and for the next five years Abe Ruef and his cronies, which soon included the once-honest Schmitz, would loot the city on an unprecedented scale.

A local political observer accurately described Ruef,

Schmitz, and the members of the municipal boards as "blackmailers, extortioners, and thieves." He added, "[T]he administration made a business of selling immunity to gamblers, prize-fight promoters, and keepers of brothels; that the great house of prostitution at 620 Jackson Street was virtually a municipal institution; that the police were giving protection to notorious criminals and taking money therefore; that the municipal boards were blackmailing law-breakers and compelling honest men to pay tribute; that the work of the city was given to dishonest contractors who divided their illegal profits with the officials who permitted them to steal."

What kept Schmitz and Ruef in power was their unwavering appeal to the city's workers. One worker interviewed said, "Skilled workmen who before the election of Mayor Schmitz were earning only from three to five dollars a day are now getting from five to seven dollars. As for graft—there has always been graft; but nobody has ever made a howl about it until now, when our administration happens to be in power. Ruef may be making money on the side, but he is taking it from people who can afford to pay; his hand isn't in our pockets." A worker's wife added, "I don't care how much they steal, so long as my husband gets good wages. They're not stealing from us."

With the ascension of labor, anti-Asian activities were ratcheted up since neither party could come back to power without wooing at least some of the workers away from Ruef.

James Phelan, for example, although out of office, called

a Chinese Exclusion Convention, during which a resolution was passed called "the character and rapidly increasing numbers of Japanese and other Asiatic immigrants a menace to the industrial interests of our people."

But neither Phelan nor anyone else could outmaneuver or outmuscle Abe Ruef. For five years, through three elections, periodic public outrage, and even a grand jury empaneled to investigate corruption, Ruef and Schmitz continued to rake in thousands and thousands of dishonest dollars and control every facet of San Francisco's political life. Those few who genuinely wanted change often despaired that it would take an act of God to dislodge the Ruef machine.

Which was precisely what they got.

CHAPTER 9

TREMORS

ON APRIL 19, 1906, the headline under the banner of *The Call-Chronicle-Examiner*, a joint edition of San Francisco's major newspapers, read: "Earthquake and Fire: San Francisco in Ruins."

The devastation was staggering: 28,000 buildings were leveled or burned out, as many as three-quarters of the city's 400,000 residents were left homeless, and 3,000 people died. "After darkness, thousands of the homeless were making their way with their blankets and scant provisions to Golden Gate Park and the beach to find shelter. Those in the homes on the hills just north of the Hayes Valley wrecked section piled their belongings in the streets, and express wagons and automobiles were hauling the things away to sparsely settled regions."

When the tremor struck, not only were aboveground structures damaged, but the city's water mains were destroyed,

The Call=Chronicle=Examiner

SAN FRANCISCO, THURSDAY, APRIL 19, 1906.

EARTHQUAKE AND FIRE:
SAN FRANCISCO IN RUINS

DEATH AND DESTRUCTION HAVE BEEN THE FATE OF SAN FRANCISCO. SHAKEN BY A TEMBLOR AT 5:13 O'CLOCK YESTERDAY MORNING, THE SHOCK LASTING 48 SECONDS, AND SCOURGED BY FLAMES THAT RAGED DIAMETRICALLY IN ALL DIRECTIONS, THE CITY IS A MASS OF SMOULDERING RUINS. AT SIX O'CLOCK LAST EVENING THE FLAMES SEEMINGLY PLAYING WITH INCREASED VIGOR, THREATENED TO DESTROY SUCH SECTIONS AS THEIR FURY HAD SPARED DURING THE EARLIER PORTION OF THE DAY. BUILDING THEIR PATH IN A TRIANGULAR CIRCUIT FROM THE START IN THE EARLY MORNING, THEY JOCKEYED AS THE DAY WANED, LEFT THE BUSINESS SECTION, WHICH THEY HAD ENTIRELY DEVASTATED, AND SKIPPED IN A DOZEN DIRECTIONS TO THE RESIDENCE PORTIONS. AS NIGHT FELL THEY HAD MADE THEIR WAY OVER INTO THE NORTH BEACH SECTION AND SPRINGING ANEW TO THE SOUTH THEY REACHED OUT ALONG THE SHIPPING SECTION DOWN THE BAY SHORE, OVER THE HILLS AND ACROSS TOWARD THIRD AND TOWNSEND STREETS. WAREHOUSES, WHOLESALE HOUSES AND MANUFACTURING CONCERNS FELL IN THEIR PATH. THIS COMPLETED THE DESTRUCTION OF THE ENTIRE DISTRICT KNOWN AS THE "SOUTH OF MARKET STREET." HOW FAR THEY ARE REACHING TO THE SOUTH ACROSS THE CHANNEL CANNOT BE TOLD AS THIS PART OF THE CITY IS SHUT OFF FROM SAN FRANCISCO PAPERS.

AFTER DARKNESS, THOUSANDS OF THE HOMELESS WERE MAKING THEIR WAY WITH THEIR BLANKETS AND SCANT PROVISIONS TO GOLDEN GATE PARK AND THE BEACH TO FIND SHELTER. THOSE IN THE HOMES ON THE HILLS JUST NORTH OF THE HAYES VALLEY WRECKED SECTION PILED THEIR BELONGINGS IN THE STREETS AND EXPRESS WAGONS AND AUTOMOBILES WERE HAULING THE THINGS AWAY TO THE SPARSELY SETTLED REGIONS. EVERYBODY IN SAN FRANCISCO IS PREPARED TO LEAVE THE CITY, FOR THE BELIEF IS FIRM THAT SAN FRANCISCO WILL BE TOTALLY DESTROYED.

DOWNTOWN EVERYTHING IS RUIN. NOT A BUSINESS HOUSE STANDS. THEATRES ARE CRUMBLED INTO HEAPS. FACTORIES AND COMMISSION HOUSES LIE SMOULDERING ON THEIR FORMER SITES. ALL OF THE NEWSPAPER PLANTS HAVE BEEN RENDERED USELESS. THE "CALL" AND THE "EXAMINER" BUILDINGS, EXCLUDING THE "CALL'S" EDITORIAL ROOMS ON STEVENSON STREET BEING ENTIRELY DESTROYED.

IT IS ESTIMATED THAT THE LOSS IN SAN FRANCISCO WILL REACH FROM $150,000,000 TO $200,000,000. THESE FIGURES ARE IN THE ROUGH AND NOTHING CAN BE TOLD UNTIL PARTIAL ACCOUNTING IS TAKEN.

ON EVERY SIDE THERE WAS DEATH AND SUFFERING YESTERDAY. HUNDREDS WERE INJURED, EITHER BURNED, CRUSHED OR STRUCK BY FALLING PIECES FROM THE BUILDINGS AND ONE OF TEN DIED WHILE ON THE OPERERATING TABLE AT MECHANICS' PAVILION, IMPROVISED AS A HOSPITAL FOR THE COMFORT AND CARE OF THE OF THE INJURED. THE NUMBER OF DEAD IS NOT KNOWN BUT IT IS ESTIMATED THAT AT LEAST 500 MET THEIR DEATH IN THE HORROR.

AT NINE O'CLOCK, UNDER A SPECIAL MESSAGE FROM PRESIDENT ROOSEVELT, THE CITY WAS PLACED UNDER MARTIAL LAW. HUNDREDS OF TROOPS PATROLLED THE STREETS AND DROVE THE CROWDS BACK, WHILE HUNDREDS MORE WERE SET AT WORK ASSISTING THE FIRE AND POLICE DEPARTMENTS. THE STRICTEST ORDERS WERE ISSUED, AND IN TRUE MILITARY SPIRIT THE SOLDIERS OBEYED. DURING THE AFTERNOON THREE THIEVES MET THEIR DEATH BY RIFLE BULLETS WHILE AT WORK IN THE RUINS. THE CURIOUS WERE DRIVEN BACK AT THE BREASTS OF THE HORSES THAT THE CAVALRYMEN RODE AND ALL THE CROWDS WERE FORCED FROM THE LEVEL DISTRICT TO THE HILLY SECTION BEYOND TO THE NORTH.

THE WATER SUPPLY WAS ENTIRELY CUT OFF, AND MAY BE IT WAS JUST AS WELL, FOR THE LINES OF FIRE DEPARTMENT WOULD HAVE BEEN ABSOLUTELY USELESS AT ANY STAGE. ASSISTANT CHIEF DOUGHERTY SUPERVISED THE WORK OF HIS MEN AND EARLY IN THE MORNING IT WAS SEEN THAT THE ONLY POSSIBLE CHANCE TO SAVE THE CITY LAY IN EFFORT TO CHECK THE FLAMES BY THE USE OF DYNAMITE. DURING THE DAY A BLAST COULD BE HEARD IN ANY SECTION AT INTERVALS OF ONLY A FEW MINUTES, AND BUILDINGS NOT DESTROYED BY FIRE WERE BLOWN TO ATOMS. BUT THROUGH THE GAPS MADE THE FLAMES JUMPED AND ALTHOUGH THE FAILURES OF THE HEROIC EFFORTS OF THE POLICE FIREMEN AND SOLDIERS WERE AT TIMES SICKENING, THE WORK WAS CONTINUED WITH A DESPERATION THAT WILL LIVE AS ONE OF THE FEATURES OF THE TERRIBLE DISASTER. MEN WORKED LIKE FIENDS TO COMBAT THE LAUGHING, ROARING, ONRUSHING FIRE DEMON.

NO HOPE LEFT FOR SAFETY OF ANY BUILDINGS

San Francisco seems doomed to entire destruction. With a lapse in the raging of the flames just before dark, the hope was raised that with the use of the tons of dynamite the course of the fire might be checked and confined to the triangular sections it had cut out for its path. But on the Barbary Coast the fire broke out anew and as night closed in the flames were eating their way into parts untouched in their ravages during the day. To the south and the north they spread; down to the docks and out into the resident section. In and to the north of Hayes Valley. By six o'clock practically all of St. Ignatius' great buildings were no more. They had been leveled to the fiery heap that marked what was once the metropolis of the West.

The first of the big structures to go to ruin was the Call Building, the famous skyscraper. At eleven o'clock the big 18-story building was flanged from every window and shot skyward from the circular windows in the dome. In less than two hours nothing remained but the tall skeleton.

By five o'clock the Palace Hotel was in ruins. The old hostelry, famous the world over, withstood the seige until the last and although dynamite was used in frequent blasts to drive

Continued on Page Two.

BLOW BUILDINGS UP TO CHECK FLAMES

The dynamiting of buildings in the track of the fire, to stay the progress of the flames, was in charge of John Bermingham, Jr., superintendent of the California Powder Works. Several experienced men from the powder works, assisted by policemen and members of the fire department, did the hazardous work of blowing up the buildings. They were rased in one of three, but the open spaces where the scattered buildings fell were quickly turned into holocausts of flame. The work was most effective in the business blocks east of Kearny street.

WHOLE CITY IS ABLAZE

At 10 o'clock last night the Occidental Hotel was destroyed by the flame which swept northward on Montgomery street and attacked the block bounded by Montgomery, Bush, Sutter and Kearny. The new Merchants' Exchange building was a mass of flame from basement to tower.

The Union Trust building and the Crocker-Woolworth Bank were both ablaze and the Chronicle building and other buildings in that block were swept by the flames.

Shortly after 10 o'clock the fire had eaten its way southward from Portsmouth Square to Kearny and California streets. The entire section fronting the west side of Kearny street.

All the building adjoining the Hall of Justice were ablaze and the firemen were striving to save the structure by using dynamite. It is almost a certainty that every building contained in the section bounded by Clay, Kearny, Market and East streets will be consumed.

The flames had eaten their way westward in the residence section as far as Gough street. There, by dynamiting blocks after blocks, the firemen succeeded in checking the devouring element.

CHURCH OF SAINT IGNATIUS IS DESTROYED

The magnificent church and College of St. Ignatius, on the northwest corner of Van Ness avenue and Hayes street represents in its destruction a material loss of over $1,000,000. The actual cost of the great building was over $800,000, but the years which have elapsed since its erection the church has been enriched by paintings and frescoes, which were priceless. Some of them were works of art which can never be replaced, however willing those interested in the church might be to meet any expense in the effort.

MAYOR CONFERS WITH MILITARY AND CITIZENS

At 1 o'clock yesterday afternoon 50 representative citizens of San Francisco met the Mayor, the Chief of Police and the United States Military authorities in the police office in the basement of the Hall of Justice. They had been summoned thither by Mayor Schmitz early in the forenoon, the fearful possibilities of the situation having forced themselves upon him immediately after the shock of earthquake in the morning, and the news which at once reached him of the completeness of the disaster. He lost no time in making out a list of citizens from whom to seek advice and assistance, and in summoning them to the conference. It was called at the Hall of Justice, as virtually the first news which reached the Mayor regarding the extent of the disaster was that of the ruin of the City Hall. He did not realize that even while the conference was to be going on carnicas would be crashing blow the structure up in the vain endeavor by this means to check the advance of the flames in the northern section of the downtown district.

All, or nearly all of the citizens summoned to the conference

Continued on Page Two.

A joint edition of the *San Francisco Call, San Francisco Chronicle,* and *San Francisco Examiner* issued the day after the 1906 San Francisco earthquake.

leaving firemen no means to fight the fires that cropped up because of broken gas lines. Desperate to halt the spread of the flames, they set off dynamite charges in buildings at the perimeter to create firebreaks. It was a disastrous decision. The explosions helped fuel an inferno that would rage for four days and leave 80 percent of San Francisco, then the nation's ninth-largest city and the largest in the West, in ruins. "Everybody in San Francisco is prepared to leave the city," the newspaper wrote, "for the belief is firm that San Francisco will be totally destroyed."

But if the destruction was unprecedented, so was the response. Even as the fires burned and refugees streamed through smoldering rubble, the rebuilding of the city began. Within days, three hundred plumbers were repairing the city's water lines, and millions of bricks and other rubble were cleared. The army was called in to prevent looting, and the federal and state governments committed the resources to rebuild. The aim was not to replicate what was lost, but to erect a new, modern city on the ruins. Such an endeavor, however, would require a good bit of dislocation, with entire neighborhoods redesigned or, in some cases, disappearing entirely.

One of these would be Chinatown.

Home to 14,000 residents crammed into 22 square blocks, filled with substandard housing and a multitude of tiny shops before the tremor struck, 4 days later, Chinatown had literally ceased to exist. Its wooden buildings had largely survived the earthquake only to become perfect fuel for the firestorm that followed.

A few days after the earthquake, on April 23, the *Oakland Enquirer* ran an article called, "Let Us Have No More Chinatowns in Our Cities," which began, "The cities in the immediate vicinity of San Francisco bay never in the past had such opportunity as now to forever do away with the huddling together of Chinese in districts where it is undesirable, from the standpoint of civilization, to permit the lower and vicious classes of Orientals to congregate."

Chinatown also happened to occupy one of the most coveted areas in San Francisco, "prime real estate . . . with commanding views." More than a year before the earthquake, a corporation—controlled by Abe Ruef—had been formed to evict the Chinese and turn the neighborhood into a residential district for wealthy whites.

Still, the Chinese had to live somewhere, so in the days following the earthquake, Ruef and his crew, called the "Boodle Boys," decreed that a new Chinatown would be built just outside the city limits in Hunters Point, an isolated spit of land dominated by mud flats jutting out into San Francisco Bay. It was perhaps the least desirable piece of real estate in the entire area.

When the announcement of the Hunters Point scheme was made, the newly formed Committee for the Relocation of Chinese—chaired by Abe Ruef—was already quietly

Downtown at Bush and Market Streets, in the Chinatown neighborhood, San Francisco.

soliciting offers for the original Chinatown land. In order for
the scheme to work, however, it was vital that Chinese residents not be allowed to return. To make certain they were
kept away, Schmitz and the citizens' committee proposed
temporarily herding all the Chinese into a tent city until they
could be permanently removed to Hunters Point.

Chinese leaders, led by the Six Companies, were determined to rebuild Chinatown exactly where it had been, but
protecting property worth millions to developers appeared
a near-impossible task. They vowed to again hire the best

white lawyers and use the courts to halt mass evictions. The Chinese consul filed an official complaint with the city and in Washington. Complicating matters for Ruef and the Boodle Boys was that no law prevented noncitizens from owning land, and so a small but significant portion of old Chinatown was owned by Chinese immigrants themselves.

Not all opposition to Ruef's scheme came from the Chinese. Although San Franciscans avoided Chinatown, tourists flocked there. In addition, many American firms had discovered a lucrative market across the Pacific. "China at present is one of the greatest markets in the world for American goods and it will be greater in time to come, and all nations will be glad to have her trade," one businessman observed. "It would not be best to San Francisco's interests to isolate the Chinese. It will work against her at the end."

But Ruef's nemesis would not be a diplomat or a disgruntled exporter, but rather a displaced newspaperman scribbling together daily bulletins. The office of the main Chinese newspaper, *Chung Sai Yat Po*, had been a casualty of the fire, so the editor, Ng Poon Chew, set up shop in Oakland and produced hand-lettered editions, which were gobbled up by refugees. On April 29, Ng presented a three-point plan to reclaim Chinatown, which needed to be "implemented by we Chinese quickly, or we will soon regret it." First, the Chinese should "[H]ire famous attorneys to represent us as soon as possible," which the Six Companies had already planned to do. Second

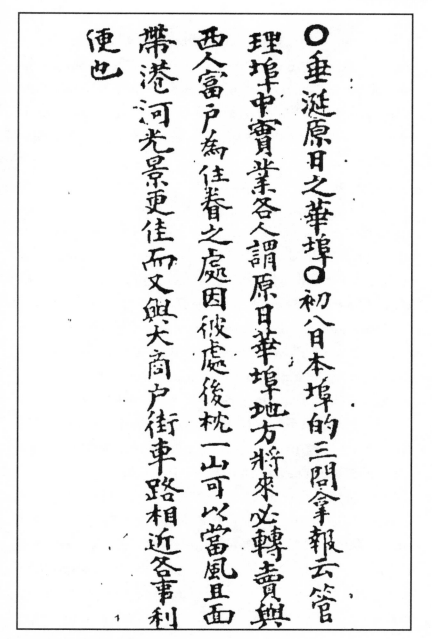

○垂涎原日之華埠○初八日本埠的三間拿報云管
理埠中實業各人謂原日華埠地方將來必轉賣與
西人富戶為住眷之處因彼處後枕一山可以當風且面
帶港河光景更佳而又與大商戶街車路相近各事利
便也

A 1906 article in *Chung Sai Yat Po* warns of relocation schemes.

was that any Chinese residents of the city who owned property should restore it as soon as possible. Third, those who rented from western landlords should ask them to rebuild and restore the lease. "Western landlords like to rent their houses to Chinese because the rent in Chinatown is higher than elsewhere."

The Chinese, for decades forced into a self-contained community where survival depended on mutual support, responded as a community, and all three strategies were implemented. In the meantime, pressure was increased both in California and in Washington to rebuild Chinatown precisely where it had been before the fire.

Under normal circumstances, with so much money at stake, Ruef and Schmitz would have found a way past any impediments, but their attention was divided. Although a grand jury empaneled in 1905 to investigate extortion of "French restaurants"—glorified brothels—could not obtain proof against Ruef or Schmitz, in the wake of the November 1905 elections, there had been a new push to clean up city hall.

Two of the few prominent San Franciscans who dared oppose Ruef, newspaper editor Fremont Older, who had originally urged James Phelan to run for mayor, and bank president Rudolph Spreckels, journeyed to Washington and persuaded President Theodore Roosevelt to assign United States district attorney Francis J. Heney, who was investigating land fraud in Oregon, and former Secret Service operative

William J. Burns.

William J. Burns to mount a campaign against the Ruef machine. Heney was honest and competent, and Burns, who would later found the Burns Detective Agency and become known as "America's Sherlock Holmes," was brilliant, dogged, fearless, and incorruptible. Spreckels, despite being warned that he would lose most of his society friends and possibly his life, pledged $100,000 to fund the investigation.

Burns and the detectives he hired began ferreting about for evidence that would hold up in court against Ruef, Schmitz, and other corrupt city officials. That Francis Heney was overseeing the investigation meant that President Roosevelt had approved, so Ruef had to be a bit more careful than before. This likely prevented him from being more aggressive in the Chinatown swindle, giving Chinese leaders the opening they needed to effectively mount a counterattack.

Chinese residents began to drift back into Chinatown and rebuild, some on land they owned, most on leased properties for which they paid high, often outrageous, rent. At first, the construction went along without an overall plan. Then Look Tin Eli, the owner of one of Chinatown's most successful tourist attractions, the Sing Chong Bazaar, persuaded other merchants to adopt a bold marketing plan. Born in Mendocino, he spoke perfect English and had worked his way up in the business world with vision, brains, and guile. He and other businessmen hired white architects to create what at least white visitors would see as "authentic" Chinese buildings. One building, for example, would be "distinguished by pagoda-like towers, upturned eaves, and a color scheme of bright red, green, and gold." Other buildings were similarly designed, and within months of the earthquake's devastation, construction was well under way.

Chinatown, it seemed, would remain exactly where it was.

Being bested by the Chinese was expensive and humiliating, and for Abe Ruef, with Burns's detectives gathering evidence against him, the timing could not have been worse. For the first time since he had come to power five years before, some of his closest associates began to question his leadership.

In late summer, Mayor Schmitz decided that an extended working vacation in Europe might be in order, and he announced he would leave at the end of September and be gone two months. Schmitz denied his absence had anything to do with the discovery by Burns's men of papers in a liquor distributor's earthquake-damaged safe that detailed a scheme in which he would share kickbacks with police officials

The United Commercial Bank in San Francisco's Chinatown encapsulates the beautiful "authentic" architecture envisioned by Look Tin Eli and others.

on every ounce of whiskey sold to San Francisco saloons. Saloons were required to renew their liquor licenses every three months, and without the kickbacks, their applications would be denied. The distributors' attorney, Abe Ruef, would be paid a hefty monthly fee to ensure that all ran smoothly.

Schmitz's denials were scoffed at in the press. "Mayor Schmitz, the tool of Ruef, is in Europe and local newspapers are quoting well known citizens, who express the belief that he will never return. A humble fiddler less than six years ago, Schmitz is now traveling in regal style, dining with princes and entertained abroad by kings of finance."

With the reformers closing in and Mayor Schmitz's return uncertain, Ruef was desperate to find a way to deflect public attention, a means to arouse his supporters to the same level of fervor they had exhibited during the strikes that had been the Union Labor Party's springboard to power. "In the municipal administration," wrote Kiyo Sue Inui, a professor at Tokyo University, "were a group who did not care to have a great searchlight of publicity thrust upon the city. They sought to shift the focus of the world's attention upon some other object."

The Japanese would become that object.

CHAPTER 10

A CONVENIENT TARGET

ABE RUEF WAS SMART enough not to further disrupt a fragile post-earthquake economy, so he chose an institution that would have great propaganda value but little tangible impact—schools. On October 11, as talk of a new grand jury began to circulate, "the School Board of the city, which was the cat's paw of the mayor and his coterie of friends," ordered Japanese and Korean children to attend the "Oriental school," a segregated public elementary school previously reserved for the Chinese.

School segregation had been proposed at a board meeting the previous year, but not acted on. "Resolved that the Board of Education is determined in its efforts to effect the establishment of separate schools for Chinese and Japanese pupils, not only for the purpose of relieving the congestion at present prevailing in our schools, but also for the higher end that our children should not be placed in any position where their youthful impressions may be affected by associations with pupils of the Mongolian race." Enforcing the order while corruption was becoming more and more public "enabled Schmitz and Ruef to make martyrs of themselves at a time when their other activities should have received the universal condemnation of the city."

The initiative was almost laughably transparent, as the number of children affected was only *ninety-three* out of a total school population in the tens of thousands. Board member Aaron Altmann, Abe Ruef's son-in-law, who had studied painting in Paris before being appointed by Mayor Schmitz to the parks commission, then moving to the school board, was said to have made a thorough study of the issue, although details of the study were never forthcoming. Instead, anti-Asians responded to criticism by pointing out the number of schools that had been destroyed in the earthquake, although "on July 23, 1906, the schools were opened with an attendance of 25,000. After a tour of inspection, the president of the Board of Education announced that there was very little over-crowding. He said nothing about the dangers of the Japanese."

But facts had little to do with the decision. The Japanese were chosen because they could be easily demonized. Japan had recently humiliated Russia in the Russo-Japanese War, routing their armies and obliterating their fleet at Tsushima Strait, after which Japan annexed Korea. The Japanese made no secret of their desire for further expansion, and the specter of hordes of bloodthirsty Japanese soldiers and sailors descending on America's Pacific Coast had already been exploited in speeches and in newspapers. As early as December 1905, William Randolph Hearst's *San Francisco Examiner* had run a cartoon depicting a Japanese soldier casting a shadow across the Pacific and over California. The segregationists could also exploit the continued efforts by the Japanese to assimilate, as they could be portrayed as worming their way into white society for evil ends. Finally, there were fewer than three thousand Japanese people in San Francisco, and likely only about one hundred Koreans, so they were unlikely to mount the sort of spirited defense as had the Chinese.

Choosing a despised but seemingly powerless target seemed just the sort of gesture that would reassure white suprema-cists that the Ruef political machine was the guardian of their interests. If Ruef thought school segregation would replace the scandal in the headlines, he had miscalculated. No one in the city seemed to care very much, and word of the school segregation initiative ended up being buried in the back pages of San Francisco newspapers. But if the segrega-tion of Japanese elementary school students seemed not all that important to most San Franciscans, it turned out to be extremely important to the Japanese, and set in motion a series of events that would resonate for decades.

Immediately after Aaron Altmann announced the seg-regation plan, the secretary of the Japanese Association of America filed a formal protest to the school board but was just as quickly rebuffed. The association then sent word of the order to newspapers in Japan, which treated the board's action as a national rebuke. One wrote: "Stand up, Japanese nation! Our countrymen have been humiliated on the other side of the Pacific. Our poor boys and girls have been expelled from public schools by the rascals of the United States, cruel and merciless like demons. At this time, we should be ready to give a blow to the United States. Yes, we should be ready to strike the Devil's head with an iron hammer for the sake of the world's civilization . . . Why do we not insist on sending ships?"

Stoked by public anger, the government called in the United States ambassador, Luke Wright, and furiously protested this stain on Japanese honor. On October 21 1906, Ambassador Wright telegraphed Secretary of State Elihu Root that the nation that was now an international naval power had been grievously insulted by the United States. But finding a potential negotiating point that would have great significance later, Wright added, "I believe it possible that Japanese authorities can be induced quietly to check the importation of Japanese coolies into the United States."

The school board had not bothered to give notice to state or federal officials, and so Wright's telegram came as a surprise in Washington. President Roosevelt, who knew exactly why the segregation directive had been issued, reportedly "went into a rage, moved to sue the Board of Education, threatened to send in troops and directed Secretary Root to cable the American ambassador in Tokyo to give assurances to Japan." Root replied to Wright on October 23, "The United States will not for a moment entertain the idea of any treatment of the Japanese people other than that accorded to the people of the most friendly European nations."

Roosevelt then dispatched Secretary of Commerce and Labor Victor Metcalf, a native Californian and former congressman, to San Francisco to investigate and, if possible, defuse the situation. Metcalf wrote a grim report to Roosevelt on November 28, in which he noted that California law clearly allowed segregation and stated, "After my conversation with the President of the Board of Education and his legal advisor, I judge it hopeless to look for any modification or repeal on the part of the board of the obnoxious resolution."

With Japan growing more incensed and reports circulating in Europe that it was willing to go to war over the insult, Californians played up the threat that Japanese people in the United States were an advance guard. In early December 1906, California congressman Everis Hayes told a reporter, "The Japanese immigrant is not an immigrant in the ordinary sense of the word . . . They came to learn our weaknesses and defects so as to turn that knowledge to their own advantage. Before Japan went to war with China, she had an army of spies and observers in Manchuria. The Japanese knew more about the Russian army than the Russians themselves. They are doing the same thing now in the United States." Shortly afterward, Hearst's *Examiner* ran a front-page banner headline, "Japan Sounds Our Coasts. Brown Men Have Maps and Could Land Easily."

Roosevelt thought such statements were nonsense and made certain his feelings were known in an address to Congress. "The overwhelming mass of our people cherish a lively regard and respect for the people of Japan . . . To shut them out from the public schools is a wicked absurdity, when there are no first-class colleges in the land, including the universities and colleges of California, which do not gladly welcome Japanese students and on which Japanese students do not reflect credit . . . Throughout Japan Americans are well treated, and any failure on the part of Americans at home to treat the Japanese with a like courtesy and consideration is by just so much a confession of inferiority in our civilization." He even suggested at one point that Japanese immigrants should be allowed to become naturalized citizens.

A few days after Roosevelt's address, Metcalf's report leaked out. Metcalf detailed nineteen incidents of violence against the Japanese, found absolutely no justification for the segregation order, and asserted the entire affair was nothing more than "an effort on the part of the labor unions to drive the Japs from the country." Pro-union forces in San Francisco responded by vowing to resist any attempt to turn them from their patriotic duty. For a champion they turned to an old ally who would press their case under extremely unusual circumstances.

CHAPTER 11

MR. SCHMITZ GOES TO WASHINGTON

WHILE INTERNATIONAL TENSIONS SIMMERED, Mayor Schmitz, Abe Ruef, and the Boodle Boys found themselves in increasingly desperate straits. A grand jury had been empaneled by the district attorney, a recent convert to good government. Its first action was to recommend the police chief be suspended, not an auspicious beginning for the ruling political machine. On October 22, 1906, Francis Heney, with William Burns at his side, told reporters, "We are going to get the crooks."

For Ruef, the only way to head off indictments seemed to involve taking over the district attorney's office, removing Heney, and getting Burns and his detectives on the earliest train out of town. On October 25, he did just that. "With unparalleled audacity Abe Ruef ordered the suspension from office of District Attorney Langdon late yesterday afternoon, had himself appointed in Langdon's place and straightway dismissed Francis J. Heney, who had been selected as Langdon's deputy for the purpose of sending to the penitentiary the graft-ers who have been preying upon the city of San Francisco." After his appointment, Ruef publicly vowed to continue the investigation into widespread corruption, for which he would have been his own best witness.

Heney's response ran as a banner above the story. "With the fullest sense of the responsibility resting upon me, I name among such corrupt and criminal officials Mayor Schmitz, Acting Mayor Gallagher, and each and every one of the eigh-teen members of the Board of Supervisors. I have the evidence to prove these allegations and at the proper time and place, as the law prescribes, District Attorney Langdon and myself, as his assistant, will lay it before the new Grand Jury. It is to prevent such exposure of their infamy that Ruef, Gallagher, and the Supervisors, in their panic fear of the felon's cell, have taken this utterly illegal step."

Ruef's tenure lasted less than a day—the following morn-ing, a judge issued an injunction blocking the district attorney's dismissal. Langdon and Heney were back in court that same afternoon questioning witnesses before the grand jury. Also in the courtroom were a bevy of glowering corrupt police officers and other physically imposing Ruef minions, making it clear that handing down indictments against the wrong people could have severe consequences.

But the pendulum had swung too far for the threat of strong-arm tactics to stop it. A suddenly aroused citizenry demanded that justice be done, and even some unions, including bricklayers and masons, repudiated Ruef, Schmitz, and the others who had been largely responsible for their ascension in city politics. One by one, Ruef's underlings were dragged into the grand jury room, the public eye, or both, and one by one they pronounced their commitment to civic responsibility and cooperated with the investigation.

Finally, on November 16, Abe Ruef and Mayor Eugene Schmitz were indicted for extortion. Ruef surrendered himself at the offices of his attorney and was taken into custody, then released a short time later after posting $50,000 bail. Schmitz, who had defied predictions and decided to return home, learned of the indictments as his luxury liner, *Patricia*, was steaming into New York harbor. He, too, would post bail and vowed to continue to discharge his responsibilities as mayor, one of which would be to attempt to deflect public anger to the Japanese. Schmitz attended meetings, spoke to workers' groups, and took up the cause of "keeping" America white and pure with renewed zeal. On December 10, for example, he addressed a mass meeting sponsored by the Japanese and Korean Exclusion League, held at the aptly named Dreamland Pavilion, the theme of which was "No Japs in Our Schools."

In addition to the racist drumbeat, the indictments also ushered in a wave of near anarchy. "When Ruef and Schmitz were finally brought to trial, the working of the 'system' became more vigorous and more desperate than ever. Ruef

THE CALL

SAN FRANCISCO, MONDAY, FEBRUARY 4, 1907.

PRICE FIVE CENTS

Schmitz and School Board Off for Washington

Brave Express Messenger Charles Is Killed in Railroad Disaster

MAYOR SCHMITZ, the local school officials and a representative of the City Attorney left for Washington yesterday to confer with President Roosevelt on the Japanese situation. The Mayor will act as spokesman for the party at the conferences in the White House.

Mayor, the School Officials and a Representative of the City Attorney Obey the President's Summons

Will Discuss Japanese Situation With Him

Caption of newspaper page.

Front page of the *San Francisco Call*, February 4, 1907.

attempted to flee. When this failed, an effort was made to secure the passage of a change of venue bill by the state legislature which would free the culprits on a technicality. Jurors were bribed; Fremont Older . . . who led the campaign against the boodlers, was kidnapped; a gunman was hired to murder him, and only the ruffian's loss of nerve saved Older's life. Francis J. Heney was shot while in court by an ex-convict who was a juryman on a former Ruef trial, and whom Heney had exposed."

During this campaign of chicanery and terror, to the surprise of many city officials, the defendants, and likely some of the jurors, the trials of both men limped along. The international crisis that Ruef had precipitated, however, moved at more hurried pace. On February 2, 1907, Ambassador Wright sent a chilling communication to President Roosevelt. "A letter just received from one of the shrewdest and most experienced observers I know, a man who sees and talks with leading men in England, Germany, France and elsewhere, informs me that there seems to be a settled opinion among those considered the most far-sighted that Japan will, ere long, attack the United States."

Although Wright did not consider such an attack imminent, he did urge decisive action to head off the threat. "This may be all wrong—quite likely it is—but it seems to me that no opportunity should be neglected to avert Japanese ill-feeling, especially as a collision would lead to very unpleasant

immediate results, no matter what the remote results might be."
Roosevelt, who had mediated the peace treaty between Japan
and Russia, was more aware than most that Japanese ill feeling
could have unpleasant results.

Two days after Ambassador Wright sent his communiqué,
on February 4, 1907, an eight-man contingent, led a by the
still-under-indictment Mayor Schmitz, with his two daughters in tow, embarked for Washington to meet the president.
The invitation from Roosevelt had been to school board members only, but Schmitz had shoehorned himself in to head the
delegation.

The president was unlikely to be pleased. "The relations
between the Mayor and the President are none too friendly,
it is said . . . The President was quoted by a member of the
California delegation recently as referring to Schmitz as the 'bassoon player.'" But Schmitz was not dissuaded—he had not only
politics, but also his own freedom to consider.

Ambassador Wright's message from Japan arrived on
February 6, a day before Schmitz and his party were due in
Washington. Someone likely told the mayor that the city's
action had placed the nation on the brink of war, because
before his meeting with Roosevelt, he told reporters, "We
have come here with open minds to hear what the President
has to say . . . It is not true that I said in Chicago that we would
not yield under any circumstances." (It was true.) "We will not
stand on technicalities if it can be shown by exercising a spirit

of compromise, we can reach results which will be for the general welfare of the whole country." He added that he also welcomed the opportunity to tell the president he was not a bassoon player.

Schmitz actually did come armed with a proposal. If the United States and Japan would enter into a treaty that excluded Japanese "coolies," San Francisco might see fit to readmit age-appropriate segregated students who were not United States citizens. Ambassador Wright had indicated previously that Japan would find those very terms acceptable, so Roosevelt instructed his ambassador to determine whether the Japanese would commit to them.

While word was sought from across the Pacific, the president of the United States was forced to welcome an accused felon to the White House and participate in discussions on how to defuse a serious international crisis precipitated by a gratuitously racist act. One can only speculate on the self-control the volatile Roosevelt was forced to exhibit being forced to seriously negotiate with a "bassoon player" he considered nothing more than a common grafter.

When Roosevelt had received indications that Japan was amenable to an agreement that would trade emigrating laborers for schoolchildren, and that Schmitz and the school board would abide by the terms as well, he decided to bypass what might be an uncertain treaty ratification process in Congress and come to an "understanding" with Japan on his own. Without first confirming with the Japanese government that such a deal would be acceptable, the president assured Schmitz that the Japanese would agree. Schmitz, who needed a win to bring home, decided to go along.

On February 19, newspapers reported that the Japanese children would be allowed to return to their neighborhood schools and that Schmitz had "received assurances that the immigration of Japanese laborers will cease." Within days, Schmitz left Washington and soon afterward returned home victorious—just in time for the opening of his trial for extortion.

On March 14, as Abe Ruef's trial was beginning, Roosevelt issued Executive Order 589, which refused entry to any passport-holding Japanese immigrant attempting to enter the country through a third-party state, such as Mexico or Canada, and forty-three Japanese children reentered San Francisco schools. Tensions between Japan and the United States lessened while both turned to hammering out an actual deal.

After extensive negotiations, in which Roosevelt informed Japanese officials that another exclusion act was possible if they did not compromise, Japan agreed to not issue any further passports to laborers headed either for the United States or Hawaii, except in the case of the "laborers who have already been in America and to the parents, wives, and children of laborers already resident there." Since the "Gentlemen's Agreement," as it was called, was not an official treaty nor a formally signed document, President Roosevelt was able to initiate the arrangement without submitting it to Congress, and even without making the precise terms public.

CHAPTER 12

HERE COME THE BRIDES

ON FIRST LOOK, THE Gentlemen's Agreement seemed to work. In 1907, the last year before the plan took effect, 30,000 Japanese, almost all male laborers, had entered the United States. In 1909, when the program had fully taken effect, only 2,432 Japanese immigrated to the American mainland, while 5,004 left the country.

But the Gentlemen's Agreement turned out to have a major loophole. Because almost all Japanese immigrants had been male, the ratio of men to women in 1907 was more than seven to one. In 1900, there had been only 985 Japanese women in the United States, 410 of whom were married. By 1910, the number of married women had increased to 5,581—almost all after 1907—and by 1920, had ballooned to 22,193. The reason for the explosion in married Japanese women was that the Gentlemen's Agreement did not restrict passports granted to wives who had been married *before* it went into effect. Anyone married subsequently could enter the United States as well. As with the Chinese, the inability to find a wife had been one of the reasons Japanese workers had returned home. Many got married in Japan and, leaving their wives there, returned to the United States to work, as had Wong Kim Ark, who returned to China to visit his wife and child. Any child born of these cross-Pacific marriages would be a citizen of the country in which he or she was born. But no longer could Japanese workers who left the United States return, so the wives would need to come to America. Any children born after they arrived would therefore be American citizens.

Arranged marriages were common in Japan, often involving husbands and wives who did not know each other, and so, using go-betweens on either side of the Pacific, Japanese men in the United States sent pictures of themselves to Japan— usually photographs taken when they were much younger or photographs of someone different altogether. Japanese women who wanted to come to America would choose a potential husband from these photographs, send back photographs of themselves, and then participate in a marriage ceremony performed in Japan without a groom. Eventually, almost ten thousand of these "picture brides" would arrive during the next decade.

Many of the women were "genuinely shocked to see their husbands. Sometimes the person was much older than he appeared in his photograph. As a rule husbands were older than wives by ten to fifteen years, and occasionally more.

Men often forwarded photographs taken in their youth or touched-up ones that concealed their real age . . . Suave, handsome appearing gentlemen proved to be pockmarked, country bumpkins." Not only were their new husbands older and more haggard than the photographs they had seen, but the men were also generally a good deal poorer and less successful. Custom was strong, however, and all but a few of the women chose to remain with their new husbands. With these marriages came children. Many children. "At the turn of the century, there were only 269 children; by 1910 the number had grown to 4,502; and by 1920 it had multiplied more than sixfold to 29,672." And so, a measure to limit the Japanese population on the West Coast vastly increased it. Moreover, to the nativists' chagrin, since those children were birthright citizens, they would have the very rights that the anti-Japan faction was attempting to deny to their parents. Thus most families became a mix of the native born, or second generation—called "Nisei"—and immigrants, or, literally, first generation—"Issei."

The effect was profound. "The growth of Nisei children accelerated the transformation of the Japanese from sojourners to permanent settlers as the parent generation ultimately identified its own future with that of its children in America. In short, the entry of women into immigrant society was integral to the process by which Japanese immigrants sank roots in American soil."

Picture brides arriving at Angel Island in San Francisco Bay, circa 1910.

Another consequence of family life was a movement out of the cities and into the countryside. Many worked for white farmers or growers, but some purchased small farms for themselves. While this worked to the advantage of individual Japanese who could afford their own land, it also further diffused a community that would need to act in concert as anti-Asian activities ramped up. One of the targets would be the very land that Japanese farmers had purchased.

CHAPTER 13

THIS LAND IS (NOT) YOUR LAND

ALTHOUGH THE REIGN OF Abe Ruef, Eugene Schmitz, and the Boodle Boys had been demolished by Heney and Burns—Ruef ended up going to prison, while Schmitz's conviction was overturned on a technicality—anti-Japanese activities did not cease but simply acquired a new set of champions. One was Democrat James Phelan, who would use the Japanese to resurrect his political career and result in his election to the Senate in 1914. At Phelan's urging, Democrats made racism a cornerstone of their program, the only party to officially call for Japanese exclusion in its party platform. But also leading the racist charge on the West Coast was a group otherwise identified with political reform, trust busting, philanthropy, muckraking, pure food and drugs (to ensure food and drug safety, crusaders pushed the government to regulate these industries and thereby prohibit adulteration and mislabeling), and women's rights—the Progressives.

One of the cornerstones of the Progressive movement was

ending control of the economy by a few massive, interlocking financial and industrial cartels. To achieve this, Progressives sought to increase competition, with controls to prevent the formation of new cartels. This, they believed, would lower prices and increase quality of goods and services that otherwise were at the mercy of the superrich, men such as J. P. Morgan, Andrew Carnegie, and John D. Rockefeller. Increased competition and the dilution of industrial control would also benefit workers, especially organized labor, which would be facing off against smaller, less powerful foes when demanding increased pay or better working conditions. The movement was often identified with Theodore Roosevelt, although he was far less an enemy of big business than he was given credit for.

In California, that formula was slightly different. While Progressives wanted to increase competition among employers, union leaders were equally determined to eliminate competition in the labor market. Once more, the target became the Japanese. "Progressives in California believed that economic self-preservation was closely united with racial preservation. It was believed that, if the Japanese were allowed to make economic inroads, it would be only a matter of time before they would make racial inroads. Intermarriage and propagation of their race would impair the Anglo-Saxon racial purity so important to the Progressives' concept of economic leadership."

From 1908 on, bill after bill was introduced in the California and Washington state legislatures to restrict the property, contract, and civil rights of resident Japanese immigrants. In January 1909, for example, California lawmakers introduced bills, among others, to force immigrant landowners to give up their lands in five years if they had not achieved citizenship, limit land leases to one year, reimpose school segregation for Japanese children, and proposed a "municipal segregation ordinance which would give cities the power to confine Japanese and other Orientals in ghettoes." Each enjoyed widespread support. "Had California been an independent republic . . . most of the anti-Japanese bills introduced into its legislature would have passed without difficulty."

But not one of them was enacted into law, nor would any other anti-Japanese bill be for four more years. Anti-Japanese activists had acquired a new set of opponents, most in Washington, but some among the very Californians they had most hoped to attract. In addition, white supremacists were at a disadvantage because, except for the West Coast, few cared about the Japanese "invasion" at all and could not understand why Californians in particular were making such an issue of it.

Opposition in Washington, first under Roosevelt, then President William Howard Taft, was based in the same diplomatic issues that had marked the school segregation controversy. Japan took insults quite seriously, and a cadre of Japanese militarists insisted that a rising world power should not feel at all averse in engaging a second western navy. Japan was a rising economic power as well and had become an increasingly important trading partner. Roosevelt had learned from the school segregation incident that anti-Japan sentiment was largely a political convenience based on overblown or manufactured arguments. He was unsparing in his condemnation of the "idiots" in the California legislature, "those infernal fools" whose behavior was "worse than the stupidity of the San Francisco mob." He was, therefore, determined to sidetrack any initiative by state governments to undermine the interests of the nation at large.

Although Taft had been elected in the 1908 presidential election, he would not be sworn in until March 4, 1909. For the measures introduced in California that January, Roosevelt, although he would be soon leaving office, and Elihu Root directly engaged California governor and fellow Republican James N. Gillett, predicting dire diplomatic consequences if the state tried to get around the Gentlemen's Agreement. Gillett agreed to withdraw his support and the measures died.

Opposition to discriminatory legislation had other roots within California. On December 7, 1908, "half a thousand of San Francisco's leading businessmen pledged the city to hold a great world's exposition in celebration of the opening of the Panama Canal." The fair, according to the organizers, was "destined even in its inception to be more vast in scope and more magnificent in detail than even the Chicago Columbian exposition of 1893 or any world's fair before or since," and would open in either 1915 or 1916. San Francisco's business elite pledged to raise $1 million just to get the planning started, a number that would balloon tenfold.

As the plans progressed, so did the ambitions and the audacity of its organizers. The Panama-Pacific International Exposition would announce to the world San Francisco's return from devastation and that the city had retaken its place among the nation's, even the world's, elite. Millions would come to see its attractions—a four-acre walk-through replica of Yellowstone National Park, a six-acre Grand Canyon, and a five-acre working model of the Panama Canal. The actual Liberty Bell was brought on loan from Philadelphia. The Ford Motor Company would set up an assembly line and, for three hours a day, would build an automobile every ten minutes. Fairgoers would watch hula dancers, ride a miniature railway or a submarine, and sit in a compartment on a swing arm that propelled those inside to and fro over the grounds. There would even be a 43-story "Tower of Jewels" decorated with more than 100,000 pieces of polished colored glass called novagems, imported from Europe and strung on wires. Fifty colored spotlights would shine on the tower each night, making it visible in every corner of what was now known as the "Jeweled City." Although nations from around the globe would participate, one of the most important exhibitions, the organizers decided, would be from Japan.

Why the Japanese pavilion was so important to the fair's

Overview of completed Panama-Pacific International Exposition grounds,
the San Francisco Bay, and the Marin County coastline beyond.

organizers was not clear but likely was based on the fascination with Japanese culture that prevailed in most of the United States. But whatever the reason, those Californians who had risked the state's prestige and a good bit of their own money on the exposition's success were none too keen to see the chances diminished by what they deemed a silly crusade against a few thousand workers and farmers.

Anti-Japanese forces were dealt another blow in 1910 when the Taft administration negotiated a commercial and navigation treaty with Japan. The treaty was strongly favored by business interests, which viewed Japan as a strong and potentially dynamic market for American goods. When nativists saw that there was no provision to restrict "coolie immigration," which would have embedded the terms of the Gentlemen's Agreement in the law, they vowed opposition. Still, the president was a Republican, as were the United States senators from both California and Washington. While Democrats, such as James Phelan, were free to say anything they pleased, Republican senators were under enormous pressure not to embarrass their party by voting against ratification.

The treaty was signed on February 11, 1911, and the terms were precisely what white Californians had feared. Japanese would have "full liberty to enter, travel, or reside in any part of the [United States] . . . and enjoy full and perfect protection for their persons and property." Japanese immigrants would also be treated "on equal terms" with American citizens in "rights of residence and travel." They could own or sell "goods and effects of any kind" and enter into contracts and protect contract rights.

Even worse, Japanese immigrants would be allowed "to carry on trade, wholesale and retail" and "to own or lease and occupy houses, manufactories, warehouses, and ships." As a result of the treaty, Japanese people in the United States were guaranteed the right to do just about anything Americans could do . . . except purchase or own land. Whether as an oversight or an intentional omission, that gap would become extremely significant two years later.

California Republicans were desperate to find some way to support their party without giving up their commitment to Japanese exclusion. The Japanese ambassador supplied the means on February 21, when he publicly promised to maintain a prohibition on Japanese laborers immigrating to the United States. Although there was some grousing about trusting the "honor" of the Japanese government, the western senators agreed, almost certainly with relief, not to oppose ratification of the treaty.

With land ownership omitted from the treaty, however, white supremacists had their next target. James Phelan wasted little time. He sent a note to 1912 Democratic presidential candidate Woodrow Wilson:

> The Japanese have invaded the central valleys of California. Take, for example, one highly productive

fruit growing valley known as the Vaca Valley. There, the Japanese, refusing to work for wages after the first year or so, bargained for a share of the crop, and finally ousted in many instances the tenant farmers by offering the land owner larger returns, and in some instances acquired the property by purchase. The white man is thus driven off the land to move farther away. The village stores, churches, and homes suffer and in many instances are left without patronage or occupants. In other words, the Japanese are a blight on our civilization, destructive of the home life of the people, driving the natives to the city for employment.

Phelan's gloomy scenario was no more accurate than the prediction that ninety-three Japanese students would hopelessly corrupt San Francisco's schoolchildren. The Japanese represented only 2 percent of California's population, and owned less than one-tenth of a percent of the state's land. An additional .5 percent, or 80,000 acres, was leased from white owners. While 30,000 Japanese worked as laborers on white-owned farms, generally for the largest landowners, fewer than 2,000 were landowners themselves.

Still, few in the Democratic Party, certainly not Woodrow Wilson, questioned Phelan's assertions. If Wilson won the nomination and then the presidency, not only would he be the first Democrat in sixteen years to hold the office, but he would have done so with help of a man whose bigotry against Asians matched Wilson's own bigotry against African Americans.

Wilson's task was made easier when the Republican Party split, with the conservative traditionalists backing Taft and the insurgents breaking off to form the Progressive Party. Roosevelt, who had handpicked his good friend Taft to be his successor in 1908, had grown disillusioned with him and attempted to wrest the nomination. When that failed, he and the Progressives mounted their own presidential campaign with Roosevelt, their nominee for president.

But if the Republican Party split was a benefit, Wilson had acquired an enemy who was anything but—an enemy who had the power to reach and perhaps influence every voter in the United States.

CHAPTER 14

FAKE NEWS

WILLIAM RANDOLPH HEARST, WHO had trumpeted warnings of the coming Japanese invasion, had parlayed a sizable inheritance from his father, George, once a United States senator from California, into a huge newspaper fortune, emphasizing sensational headlines, human-interest stories, and an only nodding acquaintance with facts. Hearst, who would later become extremely conservative, at that point considered himself a supporter of workers and the common man, the backbone of his readership, although he knew few of them personally. Politically, he identified with the Progressives, a party he wished to run and use as a springboard to becoming California governor or even president, neither of which sat well with Theodore Roosevelt, the actual leader of the party, who himself aspired to a return to the White House.

Hearst, as had Phelan, saw the Japanese as the perfect foil for his ambitions, and during the school segregation crisis, the *Examiner* ran front-page articles almost daily warning against

William Randolph Hearst.

an invasion. In addition to falsely reporting that the Japanese fleet was steaming across the Pacific, the *Examiner* wrote that coolies were really Japanese soldiers in disguise, that forty-man army units were drilling secretly at night in Hawaii, and that Japanese, both in Hawaii and on the mainland, had secreted large caches of rice and ammunition. That not one of these stories had a shred of evidence to back them up did not bother Hearst one bit. Whether or not Hearst believed what his newspapers were reporting, he thought Wilson too weak to face down the threat.

At its core, however, Hearst's antipathy for Wilson was personal. "Hearst, as a college student who preferred pranks to studies, was expelled from Harvard during his junior year; Wilson, who valued studies as preparation for service, had spent years distinguishing himself as a scholar and university president. Hearst had a 'monumental anti-British bias'; Wilson a great appreciation of things British. Hearst was noisy, rough, and self-aggrandizing in his political campaigns; Wilson, restrained, even reluctant. Hearst preferred the term 'striking' to describe his style of journalism; Wilson considered it disreputable. If these differences were insufficient to alienate the two men from one another, Wilson had snubbed Hearst by declining to meet with him in 1911."

Whether his motives were political or personal, Hearst set his enormous resources on a campaign to deny Wilson the Democratic nomination. His researchers had little difficulty finding ammunition. In addition to overtly racist views of African Americans, Wilson had little regard for immigrants from Southern and Eastern Europe; he did, however, have a sort of favorable view of the Chinese. In his five-volume *History of the American People*, when comparing the "multitudes of men of the lowest class from the south of Italy and men of the meaner sort out of Hungary and Poland, men out of the ranks where there was neither skill nor energy nor any initiative of quick intelligence," Wilson had asserted, "the Chinese were more to be desired, as workmen if not as citizens, than most of the coarse crew that came crowding in every year at the eastern ports." Although Wilson granted the Chinese had "many an unsavory habit, bred unwholesome squalor in the crowded quarters," he insisted "it was their skill, their intelligence, their hardy power of labor, their knack at succeeding and driving duller rivals out, rather than their alien habits, that made them feared and hated and led to their exclusion at the prayer of the men they were likely to displace should they multiply."

If Wilson were to overcome Hearst's attacks and win the Democratic nomination, he could not afford to lose the West, and speaking favorably of Asian workers made that almost a certainty. James Phelan, who favored Wilson but feared his position on Asians would make him unelectable, sent a telegram to the chairman of the Democratic National Committee: "Has governor spoken against oriental coolie immigration?

Charged here volume five history he favors same. Should declare against coolies as inassimilable and destructive to republican government and white labor. Answer."

Eventually, Phelan communicated with Wilson directly, and sent him a position statement that Wilson released under his own name, with Phelan endorsing it as if Wilson had crafted it himself. "In the matter of Chinese and Japanese Coolie immigration, I stand for the National policy of exclusion (or restricted immigration). The whole question is one of assimilation of diverse races. We cannot make a homogenous population out of people who do not blend with the Caucasian race. Their lower standard of living as laborers, will crowd out the white agriculturist and is in other fields a most serious industrial menace. The success of free Democratic institutions demands of our people education, intelligence, patriotism . . . Oriental Coolieism will give us another race problem to solve and surely we have had our lesson."

Despite Hearst's efforts and in part because of Phelan's, Wilson won the Democratic nomination and subsequently the presidency in November 1912. He lost California to Roosevelt, but only by 174 votes out of more than 670,000 votes cast, the best result by a Democrat in California since 1892. Phelan and his fellow Democrats were buoyed by the result, convinced they had a winning issue in a restrictive "alien land law." With Woodrow Wilson in the White House, there would be no more interference from Washington.

Their target was small—only 331 Japanese-owned farms occupying one acre out of every eight thousand devoted to agriculture—but the racists insisted this was merely the germ of an infection that would multiply and overwhelm white society. Rather than playing down Japanese devotion to self-sacrifice and hard work, these were cited as the very reasons that the Japanese would ultimately overpower whites. California Attorney General Ulysses Webb would later argue before the Supreme Court, "The fundamental question is not one of race discrimination [but] . . . of recognizing the obvious fact that the American farm, with its historical associations of cultivation, environment and including the home life of its occupants, cannot exist in competition with a farm developed by Orientals with their totally different standards and ideas of cultivation of the soil, of living and social conditions." Although opposition remained among business leaders, fair organizers, and some large farmers who employed Japanese workers, populist sentiment had become overpowering.

In the session of California legislature that began one week after Woodrow Wilson's inauguration on March 4, 1913, two bills depriving Japanese noncitizens of the right to lease or own land were introduced immediately. Reaction in Japan was intense. The *Examiner* reported that if the bills passed, "official sources" warned that Japan would withdraw support for the Panama-Pacific Exposition, and in Japan itself, "a crowd of approximately 20,000 Japanese in Tokyo cheered wildly as a member of the Diet [Japan's legislature] demanded the Japanese fleet to be sent to California to protect Japanese nationals and Japan's honor."

Wilson, as the white supremacists had hoped, did nothing except inform the Japanese ambassador that, whatever his personal feelings, the federal government could not control what individual states enacted into law and that the United States remained eager for cordial relations with Japan.

Although California was determined to pass a restrictive land law, legislators, if possible, wanted to avoid a direct provocation and appear to not be targeting Japan specifically. Militarists in Japan, although a minority, had not ceased agitating for an armed response. Any new law also needed to sidestep the antidiscriminatory provisions of the 1911 treaty. For that, legislators turned to Attorney General Ulysses Webb and Francis Heney, who, fresh from dismantling the San Francisco political machine, decided that politics would be a nice alternative to being shot in a courtroom. With his eye on the United States Senate seat coming vacant in 1914, which for the first time would be awarded by popular vote, Heney, along with Webb, drafted a law similar to those that white supremacists in the South were using to deprive African Americans of their right to vote—it appeared to be neutral and nondiscriminatory, but in practice would only apply to the target group.

Rather than specify "Japanese," Webb and Heney restricted

the right to buy, sell, or inherit property to "aliens eligible for citizenship," which after *Ah Yup*—the 1878 case in which Ah, a Chinese immigrant, applied for naturalization, asserting that Asians should be seen as white—the Chinese and Japanese were not. In addition, only "aliens eligible for citizenship" could lease land for more than three years, and corporations formed by "aliens ineligible for citizenship" were subject to the same prohibitions as individuals. Any land purchased in violation of the law would revert to state ownership.

Although publicly the bill's backers insisted that their motives were based on economics and not race, Webb would later admit, in a speech before the San Francisco Commonwealth Club in August 1913, that was not the case. "The fundamental basis of all legislation upon this subject, State and Federal, has been, and is, race undesirability . . . [The 1913 law] seeks to limit [Japanese] presence by curtailing their privileges which they may enjoy here; for they will not come in large numbers and long abide with us if they may not acquire land."

With the bill before the legislature, James Phelan once again took the lead, paying particular attention to opposition from the Panama-Pacific organizers. He "warned the committee that the Japanese are as clever in diplomacy as they are able in agriculture and manufacturing . . . [He] insisted that independent action on the part of California will not jeopardize the success of the Exposition. The Japanese are as anxious to seize the opportunity which the Exposition offers them as California is to have their co-operation. 'The future of California,' said Mr. Phelan in conclusion, 'is of far greater importance than the success of this Exposition. And in saying this I do not believe for a moment that in enacting this land legislation you will jeopardize the success of the Exposition.'"

In the end, the bill passed easily, was quickly signed by the governor, and, in August 1913, went into effect.

Questions as to its legality were raised almost immediately. Japanese leaders claimed that not only was the law in violation of the 1911 treaty, but also of the Fourteenth Amendment to the Constitution, which guaranteed equal protection of the law to any "person," not any "citizen." Some legal scholars agreed. "It is contended that the classification of aliens into aliens entitled to citizenship and into aliens not entitled to citizenship is an artificial and arbitrary selection, the only purpose of which is to prevent the Japanese from acquiring title to real property in California . . ." And so, they predicted, "The California law will in all probability be declared void, because to uphold it would limit the protection of the Fourteenth Amendment to citizens and to those eligible to citizenship."

Then there was the assumption that the Japanese, like the Chinese, were legally "Mongolian," and therefore not eligible for citizenship. Soon after the law passed, a prophetic, unsigned article appeared in a southern law journal. "The real danger [to the land law] lies in Japan asserting and proving that its citizens are entitled to naturalization under the 'privileges' of the Naturalization Act." The author cited the case of "one Akhay Kumar Mozumdar, a Hindu of high caste, a native of Calcutta, India, and a Yogi philosopher," who was ruled eligible for citizenship in a United States district court in Spokane, Washington, in 1913.

Mozumdar was "the first of his race" to be granted citizenship, and the government chose not to appeal. And so, "a high-caste Hindu of pure blood" who has "always considered himself a member of the Aryan race" was "entitled to naturalization as a white person," on anthropological grounds. Although a Japanese plaintiff might have difficulty making the same argument, beyond the Chinese, the question of just who would be considered white under the law had not actually been settled.

Nor would it be settled soon. No Japanese immigrant would bring suit questioning whether he was an "alien ineligible for citizenship" for some years. Like the Gentlemen's Agreement, there were practical loopholes in the 1913 law that could be exploited without the investment of time, money, and the uncertainty of outcome that a court challenge would entail.

Akhay Kumar Mozumdar in 1908.

In addition, James Phelan's prediction was proven correct. Although there was outrage in Japan, not only was there was no war, but the Japanese mounted a four-acre pavilion at the Panama-Pacific International Exposition, which began in March 1915, and both the fair and the pavilion were enormous successes.

CHAPTER 15

SLAMMING THE GOLDEN DOOR

AS MANY JAPANESE LEADERS had foreseen, the 1913 law turned out to be only marginally effective and loosely enforced. "Japanese farmers were able to place land in trusts and guardianship for their American-born children, form agricultural land-holding corporations, put land in the name of friends and American-born relatives or enter into three-year leases that were simply renewed for another three years at lease's end." Rather than decrease, Japanese landholdings in California rose from 17,035 acres owned; 89,466 acres leased; 50,400 acres sharecropped; and 37,898 acres contracted in 1910 to 74,769 acres owned; 192,150 acres leased; 121,000 acres sharecropped; and 70,137 acres contracted for in 1920.

Although California authorities, especially Attorney General Webb, did not announce that they would not strictly enforce the law, there are two likely possibilities why they did. The first is that despite all the public pronouncements by men such James Phelan—who was indeed elected to the Senate in

SLAMMING THE GOLDEN DOOR

1914, although with only 31 percent of the vote, defeating Francis Heney, who was running as a Progressive, and a mainstream Republican—the Japanese threat to white farmers was largely a fantasy. In fact, white farmers who leased land to Japanese tenants or sold to Nisei nominees did so at prices a good deal higher than they could get from other whites, and the sharecropping arrangements were equally favorable.

The second was Japan's entry into World War I on the side of the Allies. Although the United States would not enter the war until 1917 and was technically neutral before that, the Japanese proved to be of enormous value, especially to Great Britain, even deploying a fourteen-ship flotilla in the Mediterranean Sea to help ensure that shipping could continue free of the U-boat menace. The last thing Woodrow Wilson wanted was to have to explain to his beloved British why the United States insisted on provoking a valuable ally in the war with the Axis powers.

The niceties of United States foreign policy did not deter the German-leaning Hearst, however. On October 10, 1915, the *Examiner* ran a two-page spread in its Sunday supplement, "Japan's Plan to Invade and Conquer the United States," replete with "The Humiliating Terms of Peace Which Japan Intends to Force on a Beaten United States." The source was reported to be Japan's "Powerful and Official National Defense Association," but was actually a right-wing crackpot militarist.

123

Whether even Phelan, Webb, and the other anti-Japanese believed such nonsense is not clear, but what is certain was that their irritation increased as Japanese landholdings grew. They were further infuriated in February 1917, when both houses of Congress overrode President Wilson's veto to enact a new, extremely restrictive immigration law that exempted the Japanese.

The law gave wide latitude to immigration officials in deciding who was allowed to enter and who was excluded, and banned all "idiots, imbeciles, epileptics, alcoholics, poor, criminals, beggars, any person suffering attacks of insanity, those with tuberculosis, and those who have any form of dangerous contagious disease, aliens who have a physical disability that will restrict them from earning a living in the United States; polygamists and anarchists, those who were against the organized government or those who advocated the unlawful destruction of property and those who advocated the unlawful assault of killing of any officer." It also increased taxes paid by newly arriving immigrants to $8.

The reason Wilson vetoed the bill, however, was the inclusion of a literacy test that required immigrants to demonstrate basic reading comprehension in either English or their native language. Wilson had successfully vetoed two previous attempts to include a literacy test, as had Presidents Cleveland and Taft before him. This time with "effective discipline exercised by the American Federation of Labor and the readiness of Congress to yield to the propaganda and demands of a minority of public opinion with an overestimated batch of votes behind it," Congress voted the bill into law. Wilson denounced the requirement. "It is not a test of character, of quality, or of personal fitness, but would operate in most cases merely as a penalty for lack of opportunity in the country from which the alien came." The literacy test was the nation's first restriction on immigration from Europe.

The law also created an "Asiatic Barred Zone" that prohibited entry into the United States from a vast swath of Eastern Hemisphere nations, including India, Burma, Indochina, Arabia, the Pacific islands, Central Asia, and Indonesia. Exempted, however, were Japan and the Philippines.

Japan received the exemption, according to bill's sponsors, "at the request of the State Department because the immigration of Japanese labor is now forbidden by a 'gentlemen's agreement' between the two nations, and the Japanese embassy objected to having Japan discriminated against specifically while the Japanese government was carrying out this agreement faithfully." This was blatantly untrue, since Japanese diplomats in Washington objected to the wording of the bill every bit as much as western senators. James Phelan had tried to introduce an amendment ensuring that no Japanese immigrant previously barred would be admitted under the new regulations, but the language was softened so as not to offend the Japanese.

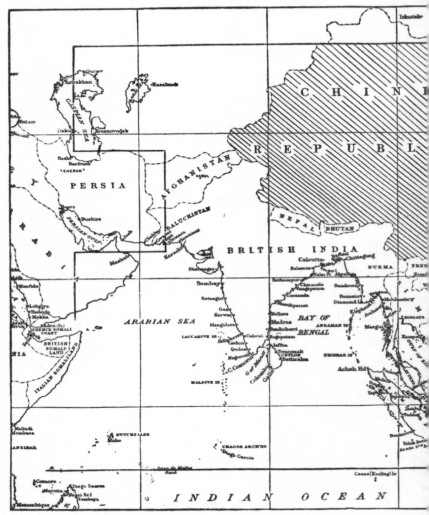

F WHICH ARE EXCLUDED FROM THE UNITED STATES, WITH CERTAIN EXCEPTIONS.

ts are United States possessions and therefore not included in barred zone.)

Map of Asiatic Barred Zone.

In California, after almost three years of allowing the 1913 land law to be openly flaunted, with terms of the 1917 public, Ulysses Webb finally decided to increase enforcement. Although the first state action was ironically against a Chinese noncitizen whose native-born partner in a land lease had died, that case was more technical than political and received little notice outside the courtroom in which it was decided. The next state suit, however, would cause a stir that reverberated for decades.

CHAPTER 16

ALL IN THE FAMILY

ON DECEMBER 14, 1915, Fulton Gunnerson sold his house at 3356 Lemon Street in Riverside, California, for $1,500. The real estate agent, a man named Noble, accepted payment from the buyer, Japanese-born Jukichi Harada, a restaurant owner, but the title deed was drawn in the name of his three American-born children, the oldest of whom was nine. (His marriage, therefore, predated the picture bride era.) Harada paid in full without needing a mortgage. He later stated "that he had no intention of doing anything but make a gift of the property to the children," and that both Gunnerson and Noble had been fully apprised of that. There was no mention of Jukichi Harada anywhere in the deed, either as a co-owner, trustee, or beneficiary in case of the children's death. Rather, whichever of the children survived would inherit the property.

The Haradas' new home was in a desirable section of the city, and they were the first Japanese family to move there. Harada later stated "he had lost one child while living in a rooming

The Harada family, 1911.

house, and determined to obtain a home for them where there was room for them to be out of doors and where they would be conveniently located with reference to the Sunday school and public school which they attended."

The 1911 treaty had given all Japanese the right "to own or lease and occupy houses" wherever Americans enjoyed a similar right. Harada's neighbors did not agree. They took "every means to oust the Haradas from the community," including offering to buy the house back for $2,000. After Harada refused, "fifteen residents signed a petition to have [them] removed beyond the tracks." When the petition failed, the residents must have put pressure on Noble, the real estate agent, because he wrote a letter to Ulysses Webb asking whether "Jap children" could own land. Webb wrote back that they could. After considering the case, despite his personal view that the Haradas had acted within the law, Webb decided to try to seize their home.

With none of the three children "aliens ineligible for citizenship," Webb's only option was to demonstrate the Jukichi Harada somehow had a legal interest in the property, despite the absence of his name on the title. Even if Webb were successful in that endeavor, he would have to then demonstrate that while the Harada house was covered by the treaty, the land underneath was not. For some reason, Webb decided not to attempt to separate the land from the dwelling and relied strictly on the assertion that the transaction purchasing the home was a sham and that the elder Harada was the true owner of the property.

Webb's case was fatally weak. Although in general, a person who paid for something in the name of another would be considered a trustee under California law, a specific exception was made for parents giving an outright gift to their children. Jukichi Harada, since he was also not listed as a beneficiary, had legally set himself outside the transaction. Webb tried to argue that because the entire family would occupy the house, the father was the actual owner, but there was nothing in the law to support that either.

Harada's lawyers, both of whom were white, filed an extensive brief that effectively undercut Webb's arguments. Although it was not directly to the point of the case, they included another argument that would become more significant in the coming years. "The question of whether a Japanese person is not eligible to citizenship in the United States is one that has never been decided by the Supreme Court of the United States," the lawyers wrote. "Natives of Japan are . . . classified as 'Mongolian,' [and] the classification certainly seems to be arbitrary. When we consider the intelligence of the citizens of Japan residing in this country, and also the prominent, powerful and respected position which the Empire of Japan occupies amidst the great powers of the world, it seems a travesty upon justice to deny the privilege of citizenship to the Japanese."

The Harada house today.

But the case was to be decided on financial, not racial, classification. Webb amended his complaint a number of times and so the case was not tried until May 1918. Webb opted to appear personally for the prosecution.

During the trial, "the Japanese counsel from Los Angeles sat at Harada's side making notes of the procedure," and "the courtroom was crowded with Japanese." Webb's co-counsel, Riverside attorney Miguel Estudillo, exclaimed to the judge that if he ruled for the Haradas, "There is nothing to prevent the state of California from becoming Japanized!" He claimed that if Harada won the title to the home and property on which it stood, Japanese immigrants would be entitled to own land throughout California, which was blatantly untrue.

The case was not decided until September 1918, and Attorney General Webb turned out to have been correct the first time. The judge found for the Haradas and used his decision to sharply criticize Webb.

> The argument of counsel for plaintiff has been directed almost solely to a discussion of the relation of Jukichi Harada to this property but has lightly passed over the interests of these children, who are defendants. They are American citizens, of somewhat humble station, it may be, but still entitled to the equal protection of the laws of our land. Their parentage has nothing whatever to do with their rights to hold property . . . Counsel for plaintiff are too well versed in the laws to believe for one moment that a resulting trust could exist or be enforced in the face of those reiterated disclaimers on the part of Jukichi Harada, all of which are matters of record.

The judge added one more comment, which must have been particularly rankling to Webb, co-author of the law. "If an embarrassing or unfortunate situation results by reason of the limitations of the statute, the remedy is not to be sought in the courts, for they cannot deny to American citizens the right to own or hold an interest in land under our laws as they now exist."

Webb fumed for a bit and then filed for a retrial, which was denied in January 1919. Feeling wronged, he was sufficiently upset to threaten to again file for a retrial, this time claiming judicial misconduct. Eventually, he thought better of it and did not follow up.

Jukichi Harada and his family remained in the house on Lemon Street until May 1942, when they were forced into internment. Both Harada and his wife died in captivity, while their youngest son, Harold, fought with the famed 442nd Regimental Combat Team. After the war ended, their daughter Sumi returned to Riverside to live in the home that was so much more than walls, floors, and a roof. She used the house to provide shelter for other internees who had returned from unjust imprisonment to try to rebuild their shattered lives.

The Alien Land Law was not repealed until 1951.

In 1991, Harada House was designated a National Historic Landmark.

CHAPTER 17

THE GOLDEN WEST

WHEN WORLD WAR I ended in late 1918, West Coast white supremacists lost their reluctance to take direct action. Losing the Harada case, while Japanese population and landholdings increased, were provocations they did not feel they could ignore.

That the Japanese had proved themselves a legitimate world naval power was fuel to demonstrate a genuine threat from across the Pacific. Before the war, many in the United States and Europe did not deem the defeat of the antiquated Russian navy as a serious peril to the United States. While both President Roosevelt and President Taft were eager to engage in whatever diplomacy was necessary to defuse talk of a sea war with Japan, each also believed there had been a certain amount of bluster in the Japanese threats. By the war's end, however, Japan, with expansionist ambitions that it had both the will and means to achieve, could no longer be casually dismissed.

One incident in particular had set off alarms. At the beginning of the war, after it had aligned itself with Great Britain, Japan had succeeded in ousting the Germans from Tsingtao and chasing the German navy from the South China Sea. But Japan had not joined the allies merely to help out. In January 1915, in secret, the Japanese government presented to China "Twenty-one Demands," which, if all had been agreed to, would have turned China into a de facto colony. Korea had been dealt with similarly in 1910. The demands were in five groups: The first two affirmed that Japan would be the dominant foreign power in Shandong, southern Manchuria, and parts of Mongolia. The third required China to acknowledge Japanese partnership in a key iron, coal, and steel industrial complex. The fourth prohibited China from conceding any coastal or island territories to any foreign power other than Japan. Each of these was simply a confirmation of goals Japan had already attained. The fifth, however—the most controversial—was new. It instructed China to allow Japanese appointees to take effective control of China's government, industry, and military. Finally, Japan warned of severe consequences if China made the communication public.

The two nations negotiated for three months. China, in no position to resist militarily, finally leaked the demands to the western allies. Both Great Britain and United States condemned the initiative, and exerted diplomatic pressure on Japan to rescind the ultimatum. Japan held to the first four, which was merely face-saving since they were a restatement of the status quo, but withdrew the fifth. In the end, the Twenty-one Demands achieved little other than warning Europe and the United States that Japan was determined to create its own sphere of influence where western powers had previously enjoyed total authority.

For the anti-Japanese faction in the United States, Japan's expansionism reaffirmed what they had spent almost two decades trying to persuade Washington. For newspaper magnates McClatchy and Hearst, it justified all the vivid warnings about Japanese warships poised off the coast of California and Hawaii, and the extreme peril of allowing those of Japanese ancestry to live and move freely in the American West. Of course, all this fearmongering was based on the assumption that Japanese immigrants and even their American-born children felt their primary allegiance was to Japan and not the United States.

One odd side effect of Japanese ambitions in China was a softening of anti-Chinese propaganda. Prohibited from both immigration and citizenship, often living in their own enclaves and seemingly unopposed to segregation, the Chinese became a more accepted presence, and even in some cases an object of sympathy for the manner in which their country was forced to endure humiliation at the hands of the Japanese.

As a result, after the war, the attacks on the Japanese began in earnest. In an attempt to influence the peace talks and gain independence, Korea had engaged in peaceful protests, which were repressed harshly by the Japanese, and thus made useful newspaper copy. Japanese occupiers were portrayed as brutal, sadistic, and merciless, which to some significant degree they were. On April 3, 1919, for example, the *Examiner* ran a story about rival publisher V. S. McClatchy's trip to Korea, in which McClatchy wrote, "In the streets of Seoul, Mrs. McClatchy and myself saw girl students suspected of inciting rebellion against Japanese rule, led through the streets by armed Japanese soldiers. The girls, some of them hardly more than children, were bound in couples by their thumbs, the lashing being tied so securely that any attempt to pull apart would have dislocated their thumbs. About their necks were leather thongs, drawn tightly into the flesh so that an attempt to escape would have meant strangulation." McClatchy was no stranger to overstatement, but accounts of Japanese mistreatment of Korean civilians were widespread, most from "neutral" sources. The article also noted that the "stories of brutality sustained" the characterization of Japan by James Phelan as the "Germany of the Far East."

Phelan had been forced to limit anti-Japanese pronouncements during the war, but he was up for reelection in 1920 and intended to ride race hatred to another six years in Washington. His campaign slogan was "Keep California White," which was printed along with his picture on placards and in newspaper advertisements. Almost the moment the war ended, he announced his intention to pursue exclusionary laws at both the national and state levels. In Sacramento on March 31, 1919, while peace terms were being negotiated in Paris, Phelan told a reporter, "During my investigations into the Japanese situation, I find a general feeling of apathy in the public mind due to a lack of knowledge of the conditions. I find the best way to get recognition of a condition, the best way to get action on the part of the men in power, is to make a noise." Phelan promised to make that noise because, likening the Japanese to cockroaches, he said, "Publicity is something they do not like; the operations of the Japanese and their propagandists will not bear the scrutinizing light. They are exceedingly crafty, working in the dark, and when the light is directed upon them, they scamper to cover."

He promised to propose a series of laws to eliminate Japanese landholding, close off further immigration, and otherwise make life so difficult for the Japanese that they would return to their homeland. It either had not occurred to Phelan, or he did not care, that for the vast majority of the Japanese, the United States *was* their homeland. They had come to America for the same reasons as his father had emigrated from Ireland for—freedom, opportunity, and a better way of life.

But granting the Japanese in the United States a measure of humanity was not going to get him reelected, so Phelan continued to beat his drum, abetted by the other white

Native Sons of the Golden West, 1917.

supremacists in state and local governments, labor unions, and media barons Hearst and McClatchy.

A number of civic and fraternal organizations were also in the forefront of exclusion, none more important than the Native Sons of the Golden West, "perhaps the most influential pressure group in the State." The group was founded in 1875, "embracing only the sons of those sturdy pioneers who arrived on this coast prior to the admission of California as a state," and was followed the next year by the Native Daughters of the Golden West. The groups were divided into "parlors," with a Grand Parlor being the ruling body. Boasting a roster of the most powerful, wealthy, and admired figures in the state, the Native Sons and Daughters were dedicated to honoring and preserving California's heritage, and in their monthly publication, the *Grizzly Bear*, members extolled the virtues of individuality, community spirit, and hard work.

But the Native Sons and Daughters were also dedicated to keeping California "as it has always been and God himself intended it shall always be—the White Man's paradise," and almost every issue of the *Grizzly Bear* contain abusive articles about first the Chinese and then the Japanese. Although no one said so publicly, both the names and the structure of the organization were reminiscent of the Ku Klux Klan. Prominent members in 1920 included Eugene Schmitz, Aaron Altmann, many of the Boodle Boys, Ulysses Webb, and, of course, James Phelan. In 1919, an up-and-coming young politician, recently discharged from the army, Earl Warren, joined the group.

The Native Sons did not attempt to hide their racism. In 1942, the Grand Historian of the Native Sons, Peter Conmy, produced a pamphlet, "The History of California's Japanese Problem and the Part Played by the Native Sons of the Golden West in its Solution," in which he detailed some of the group's history in promoting Japanese exclusion.

Official Native Son interest in the problem began in 1907. In that year, Grand Treasurer John E. McDougald introduced a resolution in the Grand Parlor calling for the exclusion of all Orientals. The resolution does not mention Japanese. The fact, however, that the Chinese were already excluded left the import of the action to be the exclusion of the Japanese. The reason ascribed in the preamble supporting the resolution was economic inability of Orientals to adjust to American wage levels.

A resolution the following year requested that President Roosevelt deploy the American fleet in the Pacific to repel an imminent Japanese attack. Other items were overt appeals to racism. "Would you like your daughter to marry a Japanese?" asked the *Grizzly Bear.* "If not, demand your representatives in the Legislature vote for the segregation of whites and Asiatics in the public schools."

Conmy made specific reference to the Harada ruling. "One of the factors which contributed greatly to the exclusion movement was a decision by the California Supreme Court holding that a Japanese might purchase land intended as a gift for his child to be given to the child when he attained his majority, and that in the meantime the parent might be appointed guardian of this future interest of his child."

Although the Native Sons and the other groups opposing the Japanese worked energetically, they often drowned one another out. Phelan and McClatchy decided nativists needed to speak with one voice. On September 2, 1920, McClatchy's *Sacramento Bee* announced in a page one headline, "Japanese

Exclusion League of California Formally Organized." The league joined together the Native Sons and Daughters, the newly founded American Legion, the California Federation of Labor, the Federation of Women's Clubs, the California State Grange, the Farm Bureau, and the Royal Order of Moose. Although California state senator James Inman was elected president and Phelan was prominently featured, McClatchy would be the league's most powerful figure. "The body will seek passage of an Anti-Alien Land Act at the November election and also inaugurate nation-wide propaganda to work for the control of the Japanese problem," McClatchy's *Bee* reported. Similar groups were formed in other western states to end immigration from Japan and to force Japanese immigrants already in the country to leave the United States.

The Japanese Exclusion League published a five-point program: cancellation of the Gentlemen's Agreement; exclusion of the picture brides; rigorous exclusion of Japanese as immigrants; confirmation of the policy that Asiatics shall be forever barred from American citizenship; amendment of the federal constitution providing that no child born in the United States shall be given the rights of an American citizen unless both parents are of a race eligible for citizenship. These were all issues for the federal government to tackle, however. Their immediate priority was to place a referendum on the state ballot to create a new Alien Land Law that would close the loopholes in the 1913 act. They sought to prohibit even short-term leases of land to aliens ineligible for citizenship, bar stock companies owned by those ineligible for citizenship from acquiring agricultural lands, and prohibit Japanese non-citizens from acquiring land through inheritance.

The league, abetted by the state's major newspapers, propagandized furiously—and successfully. The ballot initiative was approved in every county in the state and passed by a margin of more than three to one. The new law put a stranglehold on Japanese farmers, and the Japanese Association, as they had with the earlier, proclaimed the law in violation of the Fourteenth Amendment. The *Examiner* reported on the Japanese community's intention to test the law in the courts with its usual understatement. "Having made an unavailing fight Tuesday to defeat the measure at the polls [for] which considerable gold from Japan was hurried across the Pacific, the unwelcome Orientals now are scheming to invoke the courts to compel their reception here upon equal terms with whites."

The endorsement of the land law did not save James Phelan, however. Ohio Senator Warren G. Harding, a Republican running on a platform that featured opposition to Woodrow Wilson's League of Nations, crushed his Democratic opponent, Ohio governor James M. Cox, and dragged Senate candidate Samuel Shortridge along with him, although the Senate race was a good deal closer. Phelan was forced to content himself with a statement expressing satisfaction that the anti-Japan law passed. Although Phelan would never again hold public office, his efforts to promote Japanese exclusion would not wane.

The Japanese American Association would make good its determination to mount a constitutional test of the new law in court. But first, they would attack a more fundamental precept of anti-Japanese policy.

CHAPTER 18

THE HEART OF AN AMERICAN

TAKAO OZAWA WAS BORN in Kanagawa, Japan, on June 15, 1875, and immigrated to San Francisco in 1894. He learned English and enrolled in Berkeley High School, from which he graduated in 1903, just prior to his twenty-eighth birthday, having completed the "scientific course." After high school, Ozawa attended the University of California, Berkeley, for three years but left before graduation, and moved to Honolulu, Hawaii. He got married, had five children, got a clerical or sales job working for an American sugar company, and by all accounts lived an exemplary life.

In 1902, Ozawa had filed a petition of intent to seek citizenship. Although the Chinese had been specifically excluded from naturalization in 1882, by the early 1900s, courts had not specifically ruled on the Japanese. By 1910, in dozens of cases, most in the East, an immigrant from Japan had become a United States citizen.

In September 1914, Ozawa, armed with his petition of

Takao Ozawa.

intent, filed an application for citizenship at the federal district court office in Hawaii. He was the first person of Japanese descent not born in the islands to do so. The clerk at the court refused the application, citing Section 2169 of the United States Revised Statutes, which stated that the Naturalization Act "shall apply to aliens, being free white persons, and to aliens of African nativity and to persons of African descent." Ozawa returned a few weeks later, accompanied by two white character witnesses, and refiled his petition.

The clerk asked officials in Washington what to do. They instructed him to accept the application and let the matter be decided in court. In January 1915, the case was assigned to the distinguished seventy-year-old judge Sanford Ballard Dole, a member of one of Hawaii's most prominent families. Dole had been a counselor to Queen Liliuokalani, then became president of the Republic of Hawaii, and then its first territorial governor. He had been appointed to the federal bench in 1903 by Theodore Roosevelt. His cousin James Dole, the "Pineapple King," founded the Hawaiian Pineapple Company, now Dole Foods. Dole had a reputation for fairness, but also prized his standing as a member of Hawaii's white elite.

Takao Ozawa's case was heard on January 29, 1915. During the hearing, Ozawa, who acted as his own attorney, "underwent a lengthy examination by Judge Dole on points relating to American government." Dole asked Ozawa if he was a "samurai," to which Ozawa replied he was not but his brother

Sanford B. Dole.

in Japan was. "I am pure Japanese," he said, "but my heart is American." Ozawa also told the judge that in the event of war between Japan and the United States, he would fight "under the Stars and Stripes." In another exchange, Dole asked if the Japanese regarded themselves as "Mongolians." Ozawa replied, "Some of the scholars say that the Japanese are not Mongolians, but are a mixture of Malay and other races." At the conclusion of the hearing, Dole announced, "He is all right, the only question being that he is a Japanese.'" From there, he adjourned the hearing without coming to a decision.

After a series of postponements at Ozawa's request so that he could obtain more material to present his case, the hearing resumed on June 9, 1915. Ozawa, again representing himself, filed a lengthy brief. In it he asserted, "There is not a special law prohibiting Japanese from naturalization. And also there is not one supreme court decision against Japanese from naturalization. So that during the last 20 years, 50 Japanese were naturalized." He submitted a list of fourteen of those cases as well as the federal courts that approved the applications.

But the thrust of Ozawa's argument was the description of just how American he and his family were.

I neither drink liquor of any kind, nor smoke, nor play cards, nor gamble, nor associate with any improper person. My honesty and my industriousness are well known among my Japanese and American acquaintances and friends; and I am always trying my best to conduct myself according to the Golden Rule. So I have all [the] confidence in myself that as far as my character is concerned, I am second to none . . . In name, General Benedict Arnold was an American, but at heart he was a traitor. In name, I am not an American, but at heart I am a true American. I set forth the following facts that will sufficiently prove this. 1) I did not report my name, my marriage, or the names of my children to the Japanese Consulate in Honolulu; notwithstanding all Japanese subjects are requested to do so. These matters were reported to the American government. 2) I do not have any connection with any Japanese churches or schools, or any Japanese organizations here or elsewhere. 3) I am sending my children to an American church and American school in place of a Japanese one. 4) Most of the time I use the American language at home, so that my children cannot speak the Japanese language. 5) I have lived continuously within the United States for over twenty-eight years. 6) I chose as my wife one educated in American schools . . . so it is my honest hope to do something good to the United States before I bid a farewell to this world.

Ozawa made practical points as well, the most important being that according to prevailing science he was a member of "one of the four white races." The Chinese were as well, but they had been explicitly barred from citizenship in 1882, whereas the Japanese had not. He maintained that the Naturalization Act of 1790 had barred only Africans from citizenship, because the term "white" had been used only to differentiate it from "black."

Ozawa also made an ominous prediction if his petition were denied, which received a good deal of attention. "What will the United States gain by humiliating the Japanese whom our

Uncle Sam assisted to become one of the five great powers? She will only create bitter feelings in the minds of the Japanese, thus transforming a good friend into an enemy . . . The final result will be the greatest war between the European and Asiatic peoples . . . On the other hand, if the United States treats Japan fairly . . . Japanese will surely respect American people as ever before. Peace between the United States and Japan will forever continue."

The United States district attorney J. Wesley Thompson replied simply that none of Ozawa's arguments were based on the law. Thompson also filed a note stating Ozawa was morally unfit for citizenship because he threatened war between Japan and the United States. He confused "threaten" with "predict," but the Ozawa case was not one the government could afford to lose. If Ozawa was granted citizenship, it would set a precedent and "let down the bars" to Japanese immigrants in Hawaii and on the mainland.

Dole did not rule immediately but sent word that the case was so important that he was determined to give it the appropriate study and reflection. He need not have bothered. He retired on December 16, 1915, the Ozawa case still undecided.

Dole was replaced by Charles Clemons, who had been born in Vermont, attended Yale and Yale Law School, and then moved to Honolulu to practice law in 1902. Unlike Dole, Clemons was first generation and had arrived in Hawaii with the large population of Japanese immigrants already in place.

Whether his own immigrant status would make Clemons more sympathetic to Ozawa's application was not immediately apparent, but the prospect was worrisome to the exclusionists.

Judge Clemons did not issue his ruling until March 25. The day before the verdict was rendered, "a prominent Japanese" told reporters, "It would give the able Japanese in Hawaii who are thorough believers in the United States, first, last, and for all, an opportunity to further show their interest in things American. It would show to America that the Japanese who have come here to live and who expect to die here to be thorough citizens, willing to do their part to make for a better and greater nation."

They would not get the chance. Judge Clemons ruled for the government.

The decision was based neither in ethnology, which Clemons admitted was an indistinct science—although he did note the weight of evidence would indicate that Japanese were not white—nor in the "moral or intellectual" qualifications of the applicant, but simply on previous court decisions, in particular *Ah Yup*, all of which classified "Mongolians," which included the Japanese, as not "white." Clemons concluded, "The remedy lies with Congress and our alien friends should through their friends, or directly, seek that branch of the government, and if they show such devotion to the United States and its constitution as this petitioner has shown in his twenty years of complete surrender to our customs and institutions, his petition should not fall on deaf ears."

His last sentence was either hopelessly naive, or, more likely, Clemons was relieved to be done with the case. Just five days later, in an interview, Clemons advised Ozawa not to attempt to prompt legislative action until the question had been decided by the Supreme Court. Ozawa intended to press that very alternative; this time he would have help.

Japanese American societies on the mainland had hoped for a favorable ruling in Hawaii but sent word in June that they wished to aid Ozawa in appealing the decision. With alien land laws making it difficult for the Japanese to own farms— and the prospect of it being made more difficult still—the right to citizenship had become vital. Particularly vexing to the Japanese was being described as "Mongolian," which they insisted had no firm scientific basis.

In early August, representatives of a number of these societies met in Vancouver to "discuss ways and means of encouraging and assisting" Ozawa in mounting an appeal. They were successful, because one week later, Ozawa announced his intention to appeal and also that he would be represented by an all-white law firm. To fund the appeal, which would begin in circuit court in San Francisco, $5,000 had been raised, half by the Japanese societies, half by a sympathetic American pastor, Doremus Scudder, who would soon leave for a ministry in Tokyo. One source of opposition to Ozawa's mounting an appeal was the Japanese government, which was reported to have felt the time was not right for Japanese aliens to press for citizenship, although officials did not go into specifics as to their reasoning.

The appeal was presented to Ninth Circuit Court in San Francisco on June 1, 1917. Ozawa's attorney traveled to the mainland, but Ozawa did not. The hearing was predictably brief. The three-judge panel said the case was too significant for them to rule on and passed it on to the Supreme Court. From there, the case, already front-page news, acquired even more publicity. Newspapers reported that to plead the Ozawa case before the nine justices, the Japanese Associations of the Pacific Coast would approach no less than former president William Howard Taft, and pay whatever fee Taft required. Former secretary of state Elihu Root and former Supreme Court justice Charles Evans Hughes were two others the associations were said to have solicited. (Ozawa, who had studied up on naturalization law, was also said to have wanted to represent himself, but was dissuaded.) Taft declined and was forced to deny he had accepted a $30,000 retainer. Although Root and Hughes were also not retained, the Japanese Association succeeded in engaging former attorney general George Wickersham to represent Ozawa before the high court. Wickersham, a past president of the Japan Society, had a long history with the Japanese community and was sympathetic to their cause. That he took the case for only $1,000 is indicative of his eagerness to participate. With Wickersham as counsel for the plaintiff, any small possibility that the Court could simply brush away the appeal disappeared.

And with Wickersham as Ozawa's attorney, the government decided to stall, and certainly not to have it heard while the war was in progress. In March 1919, the case was put off once more. "The reason for the postponement cannot be learned," reports read. "It is considered, however, that the action of the Supreme Court has some relation to the [peace conference] in Paris, where the problem relating to racial discrimination is being taken by delegates from the Allied Nations." The case was postponed once more at the request of the government in October 1919, and then again in the spring 1920, by which time alien land laws had been enacted in California and Washington State.

Not until the fall 1922 term, with anti-immigration fervor rife in Washington, was *Ozawa v. United States* finally heard. By that time, the argument that Japanese were white had undergone some refinements. Ozawa "has traced the history of Japan for some thousands of years, carrying it back to the Ainu tribe, and no less a person than James M. Beck, solicitor general of the United States, has expressed the belief that that particular part of the Japanese race has the distinct mark of the Caucasian." Wickersham also argued that the Japanese had not been specifically excluded by either the 1790 law or any of the laws subsequently enacted to amend it, especially

the most recent one in 1906. In fact, that the 1882 Exclusion
Act had taken pains to specifically prohibit the Chinese from
naturalization was proof that the 1790 law had not applied to
any Asian, an argument Ozawa had put forth in his brief.

George Wickersham would be making these arguments
before his old boss, newly appointed Chief Justice William
Howard Taft, who had declined to represent Ozawa two
years earlier. Arguments began on October 3, 1922, and took
two days. From there, it was only six weeks before the Court
issued an opinion, and the decision was unanimous. Takao
Ozawa, the "quiet little man, working in an obscure clerical
position by, delving in the library at night," who had "ruled
his whole life and the life of his family with one fixed aim
in view," to become a citizen of the United States, would be
denied that right.

Justice George Sutherland wrote the opinion. He had joined
the court just weeks before. Sutherland, born in Great Britain,
was an immigrant, albeit from one of the "desirable countries
in northern Europe." That Sutherland did not identify with
his fellow immigrant, Takeo Ozawa, became apparent when
he took up the question as to whether the term "white" in the
1790 law was used only to differentiate it from "black."

"The provision is not that Negroes and Indians shall be
excluded," Sutherland wrote, "but it is, in effect, that only
free white persons shall be included. The intention was to
confer the privilege of citizenship upon that class of persons

whom the fathers knew as white, and to deny it to all who could not be so classified." Sutherland went on to assert, "It is not enough to say that the framers did not have in mind the brown or yellow races of Asia. It is necessary to go farther and be able to say that, had these particular races been suggested, the language of the act would have been so varied as to include them within its privileges." In other words, unless the 1790 law said "white" and "something else" to specifically include Asians, they were excluded.

Justice George Sutherland of the Supreme Court.

While it is certainly possible that if Congress and President Washington had considered the Japanese, they would have been specifically excluded, that was not what the law said. Sutherland, who generally went strictly according to language—what is now called "textualism"—in this opinion claimed to be aware of the Framers' intent, although there was no way to confirm his conclusion. None of the men who wrote the law were still around to be questioned about hypotheticals. Sutherland might just as easily have ruled for Ozawa and instructed Congress to either accept the decision or change the language of the law.

At the heart of the question was still how to define "white." If it were appearance, then Ozawa's argument of having paler skin than many of those qualified for naturalization would have merit. If it were scientific classification, Sutherland would need to choose from a number of theories, because few serious studies used broad and general terms such as "white," "black," or "yellow" as defining traits. It would surely not do to simply say that the Japanese "looked different," even if that was what he thought, which was quite possible.

Not surprisingly, Sutherland decided mere skin tone was not the proper yardstick. "Color of the skin . . . differs greatly among persons of the same race, even among Anglo-Saxons, ranging by imperceptible gradations from the fair blond to the swarthy brunette, the latter being darker than many of the lighter hued persons of the brown or yellow races." So there could be no "color test alone" because it "would result in a confused overlapping of races."

That left science. Sutherland cited *Ah Yup* and noted judges since "in an almost unbroken line, have held that the words 'white person' were meant to indicate only a person of what is popularly known as the Caucasian race." Because he seemed to imply "Caucasian" meant "European," Sutherland chose not to discuss in *Mozumdar* or another case in which "Hindoos," as East Indians were then described, were allowed to become United States citizens because science classified them as Caucasian. In another decision, a federal judge ruled that "a Syrian, a native of Palestine and a Maronite" was entitled to be naturalized because Middle Easterners were also Caucasian and thus white as defined in the 1790 law.

Instead, Sutherland observed, "Controversies have arisen and will no doubt arise again in respect of the proper classification of individuals in borderline cases," a phrase that lacked both legal and scientific specifics.

But Takao Ozawa was not a borderline case. Ozawa, Sutherland concluded, "is clearly of a race which is not Caucasian, and therefore belongs entirely outside the zone on the negative side." Ozawa would not be allowed citizenship. Sutherland did feel the need to add a final bit of hypocrisy. "Of course, there is not implied—either in the legislation or in our interpretation of it—any suggestion of individual unworthiness or racial inferiority."

Of course not.

The Court's decision made headlines across the nation. While most newspapers simply reported the decision, Hearst's *Examiner* opened its page one story observing that the Court went "far toward checking the 'yellow peril' that menaces the country in general, and the Pacific Coast in particular." Both Ulysses Webb and James Phelan were overjoyed, Webb proclaiming that alien land laws had been saved, and Phelan exulting that previous naturalizations, including those of Japanese individuals who had served in the American military—which he had not—would be revoked.

But no commentary on the case was more forceful than "Race Lines and Color Lines: An editorial inspired by the Ozawa case," written by Charles Clemons, the judge who had denied Ozawa's plea in district court. "It is absurd, of course," the judge wrote, "that a man must be either 'white' or 'of African nativity . . . (or) of African descent,' as the statute reads, in order to become a naturalized American citizen. It is absurd because there is really no such thing as 'white' person. The nearest we ever get to cuticular whiteness is, as every undertaker knows, when we have ceased to count as voters; in other words, when we are in our coffins . . . After a century or more of the United States as a haven of the 'downtrodden and oppressed' of the world, we are so mixed racially that the statutory rule of eligibility to citizenship by naturalization has become unworkable." Once again, Clemons called on

Congress to foment a "radical cure of this international ill," without seeming to realize that he could have taken a step in just that direction by putting his thoughts on the absurdity of racial classification in his decision. "How hypocritical," he concluded, to claim to be an enlightened people "while retaining so much prejudice against the mere racial 'color' as such!"

That it might have been equally hypocritical to base his decision denying an obviously qualified applicant for citizenship on a word he felt had no meaning did not seem to have occurred to him.

CHAPTER 19

WHAT MEETS THE EYE

IN THE FIRST SUPREME Court decision to attempt to come to a constitutional definition of "white," George Sutherland had more or less relied on science to make the term synonymous with "Caucasian." That seemed to bode well for another "Hindoo" applicant, Bhagat Singh Thind, whose case would come before the Court only weeks after the *Ozawa* decision was handed down.

Thind was a Sikh, born in Punjab, India, in 1892. He attended college in India but after reading Emerson, Whitman, and Thoreau, immigrated to the United States. He arrived in Seattle on July 4, 1913, before he could have fallen under the prohibitions of the 1917 Immigration Act. Thind initially worked in lumber mills in Oregon to support himself but moved to San Francisco and, as had Takao Ozawa, attended the University of California, Berkeley. In July 1918, he enlisted as a private in the United States Army, the first turbaned Sikh to serve. His unit remained in Camp Lewis,

Bhagat Singh Thind in a US Army uniform.

Washington. In December 1918, just after the war ended, Thind, by then an "acting sergeant," received an honorable discharge, his character described as "excellent."

At the same time as his enlistment, Thind applied for naturalization in Seattle as a "high caste Hindu of full Indian blood," the same description by which A. K. Mozumdar had been granted citizenship five years before. One week before his discharge in December 1918, his application was approved. Thind was sworn in as a United States citizen wearing his army uniform. Four days later, however, while still a member of the United States Army, his citizenship was revoked at the request of a local Immigration and Naturalization Service official on the grounds that he was not a "free white person."

Thind persisted, applying again in Oregon the following May. He was again granted a certificate of citizenship over the objection of the same Immigration and Naturalization Service examiner who had opposed his citizenship in Seattle. The government filed suit seeking to once again annul the certificate on the ground that Thind was not a "white person" and not lawfully entitled to naturalization. This time there was an additional complaint that Thind was a member of an Indian nationalist group, the Ghadr Party, some of whose leaders advocated armed revolt and terrorism to oust the British from India. The word itself implies violent uprising in Hindi.

There was no question that many Ghadrites, like the Irish

Republican Army, were prepared to use any means available to fight the British. Some in the group were recruited by Germany during World War I, armed, and sent to foment insurrection in India. The expedition was a disaster, resulting in nothing but long prison terms and executions. In the United States, too, the Germans recruited militant Indian nationalists, most Punjabis like Thind, to plan attacks against the British. Called the Hindu-German Conspiracy, twenty-nine Ghadrites and Germans were convicted in San Francisco in 1918 and sent to prison for violating the American Neutrality Acts. Thind, however, denied that he countenanced such behavior and produced his army discharge papers to prove his commitment to the United States. The examiner was overruled and Thind was ruled eligible for citizenship.

The government sued, seeking to annul Thind's citizenship, again solely on racial grounds. The trial took place in September 1920 in federal district court in Oregon before veteran judge Charles Wolverton. Here, to buttress its case, government attorneys raised the political issue. Thind freely admitted a past association the Ghadr Party, his friendship with its founder, Har Dayal—whom he had met at Berkeley, and who had fled the United States for Berlin in 1914—and his commitment to an independent India but denied that he would participate in or even tacitly support violent acts. Judge Wolverton was told that British Intelligence had been keeping surveillance on Thind as a pro-German, anti-British conspirator but had no proof beyond sharp rhetoric that Thind had or would participate in violent acts. Thind strongly denied the accusation and insisted his willingness to serve in the American military and fight against Germany if called on to do so, further undercutting the British Intelligence reports.

In a decision of March 28, 1921, Judge Wolverton did not give the intelligence reports much stock. "The testimony in the case tends to show that, since his entry into this country, the applicant's deportment has been that of a good citizen, attached to the Constitution of the United States." That Thind was "an advocate of the principle of India for the Indians, and would like to see India rid of British rule" did not disqualify him since there was no evidence that he had favored violent means to eject the British or had in any way violated American law. What was more, "disinterested citizens, who are most favorably impressed with his deportment . . . strongly corroborated" his testimony and "his attachment to the principles of this government."

With political objections not relevant, it was then necessary to determine if Bhagat Singh Thind was "white," for which Judge Wolverton relied on precedent. He cited a number of examples in which "Hindoos," such as Mozumdar, and those of other Middle and Near Eastern backgrounds had been granted citizenship. "It must be concluded," he wrote, "that Bhagat Singh is entitled to naturalization."

The government appealed to the Ninth Circuit Court of

Appeals, but that court, as it had in *Ozawa*, declined to rule and referred the case to the Supreme Court. Once again, the grounds for the appeal were racial—the government's brief contained no mention of the Ghadr Party. Ethnology in the 1920s was an inexact science, if indeed it was a science at all, and both sides submitted dense briefs to the Court that were detailed, authoritative, and, although neither side would admit it, totally arbitrary.

The United States attorney stressed Justice Sutherland's "borderline cases" qualification of the "Caucasian-means-white" rule, and cited this case as an example. The brief admitted there was "little ground for challenge" that Thind's origins were "Aryan"—Caucasian—but "the decision in Ozawa did not establish a sharp line of demarcation but rather a more or less debatable ground, leaving individual cases to be determined as they arose." In other words, the Court had left itself free to make up the rules as it went along.

He also stressed that in using the phrase "free white persons," the Founders had intended to limit citizenship to those who looked and acted in a manner with which they felt comfortable. They intended to exclude any race or ethnic group, especially "Asiatics," they believed could not "assimilate" into white, European-based American society.

Thind's brief sought to provide evidence that "high caste Hindus"—to differentiate them from the lower castes—had "Aryan" origins and therefore according to the law, he was "white." It was ironic that Thind sought to contest a law he contended was racist by making a racist distinction. While there is no evidence that Thind at any time in his life discriminated against members of lower castes, by his argument, he seemed all too willing to claim superiority over them.

"It may be assumed," the brief read, "that the terms 'Caucasian' and 'white persons' are synonymous," and since Bhagat Singh Thind was Caucasian, the law should apply equally to everyone as it was written.

The Supreme Court and George Sutherland disagreed.

The decision was handed down on February 19, 1923, Sutherland once again delivering a unanimous verdict. He began by quoting his *Ozawa* opinion as to Congress's motive in drafting the 1790 law. "The intention was to confer the privilege of citizenship upon that class of persons whom the fathers knew as white, and to deny it to all who could not be so classified. It is not enough to say that the framers did not have in mind the brown or yellow races of Asia. It is necessary to go farther and be able to say that, had these particular races been suggested, the language of the act would have been so varied as to include them within its privileges." Sutherland once again avoided noting that with nothing in congressional records to indicate motivation, *proving* intent was impossible. Postulating that had those who enacted the law thought about the Japanese or Hindus, they would have specifically excluded them thus became a contrivance the Court could use to define whiteness as it so chose.

As such, Sutherland dismissed Thind's primary assertion while at the same time confirming it. "The conclusion that the phrase 'white persons' and the word 'Caucasian' are synonymous does not end the matter. It enabled us to dispose of the problem [Ozawa] as it was there presented, since the applicant for citizenship clearly fell outside the zone of debatable ground on the negative side." He added, "In the endeavor to ascertain the meaning of the statute, we must not fail to keep in mind that it does not employ the word 'Caucasian,' but the words 'white persons,' and these are words of common speech, and not of scientific origin." That did not exactly square with what he written three months earlier, to say nothing of the fact that the word "Caucasian" had not been coined by Blumenbach until five years after the 1790 law was written.

But not until three paragraphs from the end did Sutherland get to what the decision was actually about. "The children of English, French, German, Italian, Scandinavian, and other European parentage quickly merge into the mass of our population and lose the distinctive hallmarks of their European origin. On the other hand, it cannot be doubted that the children born in this country of Hindu parents would retain indefinitely the clear evidence of their ancestry." It seemed, therefore, that the real criterion by which an immigrant could apply to become an American citizen was that he or she not be "different."

And so, George Sutherland ruled that Takao Ozawa could not become a United States citizen no matter how light his skin, because science said he was not white, and Bhagat Singh Thind could not become a United States citizen no matter what science said, because he did look white.

The *Thind* ruling also voided the naturalization of A. K. Mozumdar and others of East Asian origin. Mozumdar unsuccessfully appealed the revocation of his citizenship but nonetheless remained in the United States until his death in 1953, having become a lecturer and spiritual leader touting the power of positive thinking, popular with Hollywood celebrities.

Bhagat Singh Thind and his wife, Vivian.

Thind himself never gave up. In 1935, the United States enacted a law that overturned the naturalization ban for immigrants who had served in the American military. Thind applied once more and in March 1936, he returned to district court, this time in New York. For the third time, he was ruled eligible to become a United States citizen. By this time, he was "Dr. Thind," a well-known spiritual leader with followers across America. With the law now objectively on his side, the government did not object.

In 1940, Citizen Thind married Vivian Davies in a Presbyterian church in Toledo, Ohio. He would eventually lecture to more than five million people, working tirelessly up to the day of his death in 1967, leaving behind his widow and two sons.

CHAPTER 20

TURNING THE SOIL

AT THE SAME TIME the citizenship cases were working their way through the legal system, challenges to the alien land laws were proceeding as well.

Washington Territory had created the model for anti-Asian land laws in 1886, when the legislature enacted a bill that prohibited any landholding by "aliens ineligible for citizenship." As with all anti-Asian laws, the wording of the law did not appear to target any individual group, although there was no doubting the intent. There had been other proposals that year, including one that would not have allowed immigrants ineligible for citizenship to run laundries, but territorial officials thought they might be a little *too* obvious. When Washington attained statehood in 1889, it replaced the 1886 law with a constitutional provision altering the prohibition to immigrants who had not declared their intention to become United States citizens, something the legally barred Chinese could not do.

As in California, the Japanese population in Washington

grew, rising from 5,617 in 1900 to 12,929 in 1910, to more than 15,000 in 1920, and they replaced the Chinese as the main target of anti-Asian bigotry. Although the number of Japanese farmers was relatively small, "the Japanese, through his skill and effort, had won an important place for himself in the agricultural market."

Also as in California, however, the constitutional provision in Washington had sufficient loopholes to render it largely ineffective. Japanese farmers could either lease land from whites or purchase land through corporations owned on paper by white trustees, usually the purchaser's attorneys. To close the loopholes, Washington enacted an alien land law in 1921 modeled after the California law of 1920.

In order not to discourage foreign nationals—Europeans—from investing in the state, the law did "not include lands containing valuable deposits of minerals, metals, iron, coal or fire clay" or "the necessary land for mills and machinery to be used in development." Although the provision read "an alien who had not declared, in good faith, his intention of becoming a citizen," rather than simply "an alien ineligible for citizenship." Japanese were not eligible for citizenship and therefore could not apply in good faith.

Anyone who leased land to barred immigrants would forfeit title and be subject to one year in jail. In July 1921, soon after the law was enacted, Frank Terrace and his wife, Elizabeth, along with N. Nakatsuka (no other name was given) brought suit to prevent Lindsay Thompson, Washington's attorney general, from enforcing that provision since Terrace wished to lease a part of his land to Nakatsuka. The suit was financed by the Northwest American Japanese Association and was brought in federal rather than state court, since the challenge was to be on Fourteenth Amendment grounds.

Judge Edward Cushman, who would hear the case, was a close associate of Congressman Albert Johnson, an outspoken anti-Semite, white supremacist, and would-be sponsor of the most restrictive immigration law in American history. Cushman, to no one's surprise, refused the Terraces and dismissed constitutional questions out of hand.

Terrace and Nakatsuka appealed to the Supreme Court, which heard the case in April 1923. They claimed a denial of due process and equal protection guarantees of the Fourteenth Amendment grounds, and secondarily that the Washington law interfered with treaty obligations. The Terraces also pointed out that they had acquired their property at a time when it could lawfully be leased to Japanese persons. Washington had therefore denied them the right to use their property in a lawful way and dispose of it as they chose. Property rights had been used successfully before the Court in cases where civil rights would have been ignored.

Washington's reply was that the case had nothing to do with equal protection of the laws but rather the right of the state to protect its citizens from foreign infestation, "that the public welfare is directly affected by the alien ownership of realty." And how could people in the East know how dangerous these devious "aliens" were? "The most drastic action in this regard has been taken by those States in which there are found large bodies of aliens who are not permitted by Congress to become naturalized."

And the risk, according to Washington, was severe. "In the field of agriculture, the American and Oriental cannot compete. The possible result of such a condition would be that in the course of time, in certain sections of the country, at least, all lands might pass to these classes of aliens. The people of the State would then be entirely dependent for their very existence upon alien races who recognize to the State or Nation no other obligations than those forcibly imposed." Once again, the Japanese were to be penalized for showing the very commitment to success that in whites was considered virtuous.

On November 12, 1923, by a 6–0 vote, the Court bowed to the judgment of the state. The reasoning was tortured and the decision transparently racist. Pierce Butler, for the majority, wrote that the law had not targeted specific races, despite the fact that the state's brief had made no secret that it had. "Appellants' contention that the state act discriminates arbitrarily against Nakatsuka and other ineligible aliens because of their race and color is without foundation. All persons of whatever color or race who have not declared their intention in good faith to become citizens are prohibited from so owning agricultural lands."

Butler continued the charade by observing that there are

always two classes of aliens, those eligible for citizenship and those who are not, as if the question of race did not exist. And so, "The Terraces, who are citizens, have no right safeguarded by the Fourteenth Amendment to lease their land to aliens lawfully forbidden to take or have such lease."

With the Washington law upheld, the Court turned its attention to California. The same day the Court issued the opinion in Terrace, it ruled in *Porterfield v. Webb* that a similar provision

A Japanese family, the Hamadas, in their orchard in Parkdale, Oregon, circa 1920.

of the 1920 California law was neither in violation of the 1911 treaty nor the Fourteenth Amendment. That the California law was broader in that it made no distinction between ineligible immigrants who voiced an intention to become citizens and those who had not was not an important distinction. Pierce Butler again wrote the opinion and was joined by the same justices who had concurred in Terrace.

Ulysses Webb, attorney general of California.

One week later, November 19, 1923, the Court decided two more challenges to the California law. In *Webb v. O'Brien*, the justices, aligned exactly as in the previous cases, overturned a district court ruling that a sharecropping arrangement was not an employment contract but rather gave the lessee, a Japanese man named Inouye, "a capable farmer," an interest in the land "substantially similar to that granted to a lessee." In the fourth case, *Frick v. Webb*, Pierce Butler writing for the same majority, agreed that a state may "forbid indirect as well as direct ownership and control of agricultural land by ineligible aliens" and ban immigrants from owning stock in landholding corporations.

The four decisions taken together were crushing. They eliminated any possibility that as citizens or noncitizens, Japanese Americans could succeed in working their way into the fabric of American life. Had the decisions been different, in time, whites may have come to see the Japanese as valued members of their communities instead of as outsiders to be feared and loathed. By contriving their decisions to conform to race prejudice, the Supreme Court did a grave disservice to white society as well as to the Japanese.

CHAPTER 21

BANZAI AND BASEBALL

THE FOLLOWING YEAR, 1924, marked the high point for race prejudice in the United States. That year, after decades of lobbying, with African Americans living under Jim Crow rule in the South and herded into ghettos in the North, white supremacists achieved their most coveted goal. Congress passed and President Calvin Coolidge signed the Johnson-Reed Act, the most sweeping anti-immigration legislation ever enacted in the United States.

The literacy test in the 1917 law had not been as effective as planned in barring "undesirables," especially those from Southern and Eastern Europe, so nativists had moved to a conveniently formulated quota system based on nation of origin. The quota was set at 2 percent of the total number of people of each nationality in the United States as of the 1890 census. They used 1890 instead of a later census because the numbers most favored immigrants from northwest Europe, who were deemed of superior white Nordic stock.

Samuel Gompers.

Once again, organized labor, spearheaded by an immigrant, Samuel Gompers, head of the American Federation of Labor, had lent crucial support to the bill as a vehicle for restricting cheap labor. Gompers tried to portray those who favored an intentionally unfair quota system as victims. "The report of the [A.F. of L.'s] legislative committee," newspaper reports read, "declares that the Johnson immigration bill, providing for a two per cent quota and the admission of families of foreign-born citizens, is being 'maliciously attacked in foreign countries, by their nationals in the United States' and by 'unfair and greedy corporations.'"

Although for much of the nation, the anti-immigration movement had focused on Southern and Eastern Europe, westerners, led once more by James Phelan and V. S. McClatchy, demanded the legislation include a provision that would end all immigration from Japan. McClatchy in particular, furious about picture brides and the *Harada* decision, had written a series of editorials in his newspaper, the *Sacramento Bee*, complaining of the Japanese "astronomical birth rate," and

A May 1920 headline in a McClatchy newspaper denouncing a pastor who opposed exclusion.

"increased landholding" as threats to Anglo-Saxon civilization. "They come here specifically and professedly," he wrote, "for the purpose of colonizing and establishing here permanently the proud Yamato race." McClatchy and his fellows would also have preferred the law provide for a means to evict Japanese noncitizens already in the United States, but the legal problems were seen to be insurmountable.

To satisfy this increasingly important voting bloc, a provision of the Johnson-Reed Act specifically barred all immigration from South and East Asia, this time including Japan, putting the Japanese (and Koreans) on the same footing as the post-1882 Chinese. Although Japanese diplomats protested vigorously, and President Calvin Coolidge, fearing the safety of Christian missionaries in Japan, urged either an exception for Japan or a delay in implementation, Congress refused to alter the bill. The final version passed with veto-proof majorities—69–9 in the Senate and 308–58 in the House. With no alternative, Coolidge dutifully signed the bill into law.

Although the Johnson-Reed Act had the desired effect in choking off new immigration, the Japanese population in the United States almost doubled between 1910 and 1930, topping out at almost 140,000. In addition, American-born Japanese were getting older, many approaching their teens, and like current DACA children, identified solely as Americans. Many spoke little or no Japanese. Nisei would eventually attend American universities and aspire, as did every other immigrant group, to use their parents' work in the fields and factories as a springboard to a better life. But as the American dream grew among the Nisei, race hatred by whites grew right along with it. They were convinced that the Japanese living in the United States, even those who had been born there, held a primary allegiance to Japan and constituted a threat not just to American workers but also to American national security.

The situation was complicated by enormous political and social changes in Japan itself. On the one hand, there was a rise of militarism and extreme nationalism, advocating a return to the samurai culture. The Japanese military had been influential in the government since the Meiji Restoration and had become even more powerful after the great victory against Russia in 1905. Not until the late 1920s, however, did military leaders begin a push to officially run the government. To the militarists, the exclusion of Japanese immigrants to the United States on racial grounds was an unforgivable insult.

In 1931, to gain access to the iron and coal it lacked at home, Japan overran the Chinese province of Manchuria and installed a puppet government. In July 1937, Japanese forces succeeded in occupying almost the entire east coast of China, during which they committed severe and widely publicized atrocities against the Chinese population, especially during the fall of Nanking. The barbarism of the Japanese military received wide coverage in the American press and reinforced racial stereotypes in the United States all the more. American military and political officials became alarmed that Japanese ambitions might threaten Hawaii and even the American West Coast.

With President Roosevelt's approval, the FBI and the Office of Naval Intelligence (ONI) began to formulate lists of potential Japanese agents living in the western United States. By 1940, the list had grown to almost five thousand names from California alone. The methodology by which the lists were compiled, however, was questionable. "Members of Japanese businesses and cultural organizations, including Shinto and Buddhist priests, were classified as potential spies or saboteurs." Again urged on by West Coast white supremacists, many government leaders in Washington became convinced that the Japanese in the United States were secretly taking orders from anti-American leaders in Japan and were preparing to attack as soon as they received word to do so.

But most Americans were also well aware of a growing fascination with American culture in Japan, much of it centering on what was fast becoming the Japanese national game—baseball. "In 1931 and 1934, elite major league players barnstormed across Japan, playing for the first time against all-Japanese teams. And in 1935, Japan's first professional baseball team visited the United States and competed against minor league clubs from California to Ohio. Writers depicted a Japan that esteemed and excelled at America's 'national game.' Americans read how Japanese people poured into city streets and packed modern stadiums to catch a glimpse of icons like Babe Ruth. Others personally saw Japanese ballplayers deftly turn double plays and bow to umpires in small cities like Pocatello, Idaho, and Madison, Wisconsin. Writers and diplomats alike spoke of shared values . . . Such overt enthusiasm for the 'democratic' raised profound questions about the nature of Japanese people and society."

Both of these strains bore on the treatment of Japanese Americans through the 1930s. Many in the white population who thought of the Chinese as a "foreign" race decided perhaps that the Japanese in the United States were different. They worked hard at being "American," trying to integrate themselves into the wider—and whiter—population without forcing themselves on those who thought them pariahs. But even among their most fervent supporters there lurked a suspicion that some, perhaps even many, in the Japanese community harbored a secret loyalty to Japan that would present a grave risk to American security if war came.

When war did come, both of these forces initially came into play, before bigotry and fear overwhelmed tolerance and common sense. And so began one of the most shameful episodes in United States' history.

A team of elite American baseball players visited Japan in 1934, including Babe Ruth, pictured here with young Japanese players; Lou Gehrig; and other Hall of Famers.

CHAPTER 22

FEAR AND FICTION

AT 7:55 A.M. ON December 7, 1941, Japan began its attack on American forces at Pearl Harbor. They used more than three hundred torpedo planes, bombers, dive-bombers, and fighters launched from four aircraft carriers. Their attack fleet also included more than fifty additional warships, from battleships to midget submarines to oilers. In 1 hour and 15 minutes, 2,335 United States military personnel and 68 civilians were dead—almost half Japanese fishermen—and more than 1,000 were wounded. Nineteen ships, including eight battleships, were either destroyed or heavily damaged. Only because three aircraft carriers were out to sea was some of the Pacific Fleet salvaged.

December 7, 1941, is one of the most important dates in American history. The Pearl Harbor attack not only propelled the nation into a war most Americans had been desperate to avoid but also told Americans that even two oceans could not insulate them from world events. The United States changed overnight from a country that could learn of death and destruction around the world without feeling a personal threat to one that would harness its immense resources in a fight that had suddenly become personal.

Almost from the moment the last Japanese plane was returning to an aircraft carrier, military, civilian, and government agencies were on a war footing. As President Roosevelt was asking Congress for a declaration of war, battle plans were redrawn, reservists were called up, factories ordered converted to war production, newspaper reporting was restricted, blackouts were imposed—and Japanese Americans on the West Coast were arrested.

Although both the FBI and ONI had used their questionable lists of potential Japanese agents to target those to be arrested, there was extensive evidence that not only were Japanese Americans almost universally loyal to the United States, but that authorities in Japan thought them traitors because they had abandoned Japan for America. One of President Roosevelt's "private spies" reported in November 1941 that in case of war, "there was no danger of widespread anti-American activities" from the Japanese and that they "were in more danger from whites than the other way around." The agent added, "The Nisei are pathetically eager to show loyalty. They are not Japanese in culture. They are foreigners to Japan."

Although wild rumors flew about that the Japanese were

planning an imminent attack on the West Coast, or had already attacked, for almost a month after Pearl Harbor, many California newspapers and even state officials called for calm, insisting that most Japanese residents were loyal Americans who wanted nothing more than to aid their nation in a time of war. In schools up and down the coast, both teachers and students made an effort to reassure their Japanese schoolmates that their loyalty was not in question.

But such sentiments were soon swept away by a combination of fact, fiction, rumor, and just plain bad luck. The fact was that the Japanese military was sweeping across the Pacific, overwhelming overmatched foes with a combination of relentless attack and hideous brutality. By mid-February 1942, they would conquer the "impregnable" British stronghold in Singapore and threaten Australia, as well as Hawaii.

The fiction was that a campaign of sabotage within the United States was already under way. Japanese farmers were said to have embarked on a campaign to poison the food and water supplies, and Japanese fishermen were actually naval officers, waiting for a signal to attack American warships as they lay at anchor. There were vivid descriptions of nonexistent bombings or attacks on military installations. The scope of the reports, not one of which proved true, was astonishing but nonetheless, by their volume alone, seemed to American leaders in Washington, DC, three thousand miles away, to be at least somewhat reflective of the actual situation.

The bad luck was that the officer in charge of the Western Command, General John DeWitt, a talentless bureaucrat who had served in the army for more than forty years without ever commanding a combat unit, believed just about every outrageous report or rumor that came across his desk. DeWitt was an ignorant, narrow-minded bigot who was convinced he needed to save the nation from loathsome foreigners who were bent on destroying it. "A Jap is a Jap," he regularly remarked, and he would tell a subordinate, "There isn't such a thing as a loyal Japanese, and it is just impossible to determine their loyalty by investigation—it just can't be done."

The bad luck was compounded because DeWitt's second in command was General Joseph W. "Vinegar Joe" Stilwell, who was highly intelligent, totally competent, and convinced that the rumors to which DeWitt gave so much credence were utter nonsense. In his diary, he referred to DeWitt as a "jackass." Had the order of command been reversed, history might have been far different. As it was, Stilwell soon left for Washington to help plan an invasion of North Africa and DeWitt was left to peddle his conspiracy theories to senior military and political officials, including President Roosevelt. The only way to secure the West Coast, DeWitt told anyone who would listen, was to clear the Japanese out.

Into this increasingly incendiary brew leapt California's ambitious attorney general and future governor, Earl Warren. Although he would come to deeply regret his actions, Warren

Earl Warren in military uniform.

became perhaps the most influential civilian voice in support of DeWitt's initiative.

One of the most persistent rumors was that the Japanese would launch attacks and acts of sabotage from their homes and farms. Under Warren's direction, an official in each county was assigned to locate and map all Japanese-occupied land and compare it with "important installations" in the vicinity. When the survey was complete, Warren forwarded the results to the army, although the exercise was absurd because just about everyone in California lived near something that would qualify as an "important installation." In his transmittal, Warren concluded, "The Japanese situation as it exists in California today may well be the Achilles heel of the entire civilian defense effort. Unless something is done, it may bring about a repetition of Pearl Harbor."

But Roosevelt remained uncertain. Agents he had sent to the West Coast had assured him that Japanese Americans were no threat. To get a firsthand picture, in January 1942, the House of Representatives Select Committee Investigating National

Defense Migration traveled to San Francisco for special hearings. Warren testified that he was convinced that the "distribution of the Japanese population appears to manifest something more than coincidence." Japanese Americans, he added, were "ideally situated with reference to points of strategic importance, to carry into execution a tremendous program of sabotage on a mass scale should any considerable number of them be inclined to do so." The congressmen were suitably impressed, although it turned out that Warren's definition of "strategic installation" had been contrived to suit his conclusions.

And so, on February 19, 1942, President Roosevelt signed Executive Order 9066. Like most discriminatory government actions, Roosevelt's pretended to be race neutral. It authorized the removal from designated zones on the West Coast of anyone deemed a threat by the military authorities—or General Dewitt—in the area. In practice, as everyone knew, this would apply only to the Japanese. DeWitt took the order one step further and rather than removing Japanese residents on an individual basis, declared the West Coast an area of exclusion, allowing him to sweep up more than one hundred thousand Americans without trial or legal procedure of any kind.

Even before DeWitt began to institute the mass relocations, thousands of Japanese Americans, most of them Issei, had already been taken into custody, including doctors, lawyers, and prominent businessmen. Many of those had seen

A sign on a Japanese grocery store in California. It did not save the family from relocation.

their homes ransacked, their possessions manhandled or destroyed, their businesses ruined, and, in some cases, their land or farms sold for virtually nothing to eager speculators. As one white farmer said, "We're charged with wanting to get rid of the Japs for selfish reasons. We do. It's a question of whether the white man lives on the Pacific Coast or the brown men. They came into this valley to work, and they stayed to take over. If all the Japs were removed tomorrow, we'd never miss them in two weeks because the white farmers can take over and produce everything the Jap grows. And we do not want them back when the war ends, either."

CHAPTER 23

NO ISLAND PARADISE

IN HAWAII, IN THE days after Pearl Harbor, more than 2,500 Japanese Americans were arrested. They included business and community leaders, even Buddhist monks—anyone who had been on an FBI or ONI list of potential subversives. But the situation on the islands was different from on the American mainland. Approximately one-third of Hawaii's 450,000 residents were either Issei or Nisei, and a mass relocation would devastate the economy. In addition, with a massive increase in military personnel expected, the lack of Japanese civilian workers would cause chaos.

Still, fear of an imminent Japanese invasion weighed heavily in Washington, especially since many in government thought the Japanese military would be aided by disloyal Japanese Americans. The invasion scare, at least, was real. "Admiral Isoroku Yamamoto, the architect of the Pearl Harbor attack, planned to annihilate American aircraft carriers at the Battle of Midway and then seize the Hawaiian Islands and use their civilian population of over 460,000 as a bargaining chip to secure a quick negotiated peace." (The Japanese would be dealt a crushing defeat at Midway in June 1942, so Yamamoto's strategy would never be tested.)

Although there was not a shred of evidence that the Japanese population in Hawaii was anything less than fiercely loyal Americans, on March 13, 1942, weeks after he signed the order authorizing relocations on the West Coast, President Roosevelt signed an order that could have resulted in the same treatment of Japanese Americans in the islands. But the army commander, General Delos Emmons, was no John DeWitt. He knew that hysteria was not a reason to abandon sound judgment. Although almost two thousand Japanese were eventually sent to the mainland for internment and a small number were interned on the islands, the vast majority were allowed to remain in their homes.

But that does not mean they were well treated. Hawaii was placed under martial law with legal guarantees suspended. Japanese residents were not allowed to travel more than ten miles from their homes, nor to change jobs or residences, without approval from the army. Soldiers conducted random searches without warrants of the homes of Japanese citizens looking for anything that might signal disloyalty.

There were curfews and blackouts that were strictly enforced. "At the Puna Hongwanji temple, American soldiers shot their rifles at a flashing light in the tower after one insisted it was a spy sending coded light signals to the Japanese in violation of the blackout regulations. Explaining that the tower was a columbarium where the deceased members' ashes were kept, a lay Buddhist member of the temple led the soldiers up the stairs, where they found a large mirror, reflecting the moonlight."

Japanese people were forbidden to own boats and so fishermen could not work. Others were barred from certain jobs and were not allowed to teach school. Many Nisei were required to wear black badges issued by the army, on which the word RESTRICTED was printed. Anyone wearing such a badge could not work in areas designated as "sensitive" by the military. All activities considered "un-American" were targeted, including religion. "The Office of the Military Governor's official policy was to 'discourage Japanese religious activities other than Christian,'" and Buddhists were "encouraged" to attend Christian churches.

Although only a small number of Japanese were interned in Hawaii, even free Japanese Americans were never allowed to forget they were considered enemies of the country.

CHAPTER 24

INFAMY

ALTHOUGH ONE OF THE clauses in Executive Order 9066 stipulated that deportees be provided "food, shelter, and other accommodations as may be necessary," no facilities on the mainland existed to house 100,000 men, women, and children. To comply with the order, the Army Corps of Engineers set to converting race tracks and athletic stadiums to temporary holding facilities while crude housing, "tar paper-covered barracks of simple frame construction without plumbing or cooking facilities of any kind," was thrown up by private contractors in more than a dozen locations, mostly in barren, isolated sections of the West.

To fill these ghastly camps, all Americans of Japanese descent, whether or not they were citizens, were required to register for relocation. This alone was a gross humiliation, but there was far worse to come. Each of those who had registered was given notice to report to a train or bus station, with only those scant possessions they could carry, some of which

Deported family of Japanese ancestry waiting to board a train.

Tule Lake internment camp for Japanese Americans in Newell, California.

would be lost or destroyed by soldiers who considered them enemy prisoners of war. When the time came to report for debarkation, most Japanese Americans acquiesced and came to the appointed areas to be herded onto buses or railroad cars and taken to barbed-wire-enclosed compounds in parts of the nation in which few white people thought fit to live. Most would remain there for three years.

During that time, these "concentration camps," as they were called by the authorities that managed them, would be home to innocent, loyal Americans, including the families of American soldiers who died or were decorated for bravery fighting for the country that had treated them so unfairly.

The conditions at the camps were appalling. In some cases, Japanese families were forced to live in what had been stalls for horses. American citizens accused of no crimes had been deported to:

> spare, prison-like compounds situated on sunbaked deserts or bare Ozark hillsides, dotted with watchtowers and surrounded by barbed wire. The sites of the camps—Topaz in Utah, Minidoka in Idaho, Gila River and Poston in Arizona, Heart Mountain in Wyoming, Amache in Colorado, Rohwer and Jerome in Arkansas, and Tule Lake and Manzanar in California—had been chosen for their remoteness, and for most internees they must have seemed as alien as the surface of the moon. Life in the camps had a

military flavor; internees slept in barracks or small compartments with no running water, took their meals in vast mess halls, and went about most of their daily business in public.

Most Japanese people in the camps tried desperately to create some semblance of normal life, especially for children. They set up schools, athletic activities, published camp newspapers—strictly censored by the army—and had even a police force and jails. The more the internees tried to make life seem normal, however, the more it was clear that it was not. Military authorities encouraged these "Americanization programs," and "Japanese Americans who cooperated with the programs were rewarded while those who resisted were isolated and labeled as 'troublemakers.'"

Those troublemakers were sent to Tule Lake in northern California, near the Oregon border. While the physical conditions at Tule Lake were not substantially worse than at many of the other camps, those assigned were considered little more than prisoners of war and were constantly harassed and denied even minimal civil liberties. That it was only the exercise of constitutionally guaranteed civil liberties that got an internee transferred to Tule Lake seemed lost on the War Department, Congress, and the White House.

What was remarkable was that unspeakable treatment did not cause the internees to turn against the country that had treated them so shabbily. Instead, many Japanese internees shamed the

Behind barbed wire.

Official announcement of the formation of a combat regiment to be made up of 1,500 Americans of Japanese ancestry was the signal for hundreds of loyal citizens in Hawaii to go to their draft boards and sign up.

nation with their patriotism. In 1943, the War Department finally decided that native-born Americans of Japanese descent were perhaps not "enemy aliens" and were eligible to participate in the war effort. Not in the Pacific, of course—Japanese Americans could not be trusted *that* much. But the army asked for volunteers for a unit to be assigned to Europe. Almost immediately thousands of young men from both Hawaii and the mainland volunteered. The 442nd Regimental Combat Team, composed of these volunteers, was sent to Italy and fought with astonishing bravery, with more than eight hundred dying for their country and hundreds more wounded.

The 442nd also became the most decorated unit for its size in the entire United States Army. "They won seven Distinguished Unit Citations, including one awarded personally by President Harry Truman who said, on July 15, 1946, 'You fought the enemy abroad and prejudice at home and you won.' In addition, after an exhaustive survey of individual actions from WWII, twenty more Medals of Honor were awarded, bringing the total to twenty-one. Over 4,000 Purple Hearts, 29 Distinguished Service Crosses, 588 Silver Stars, and more than 4,000 Bronze Stars were awarded to the men of the 442nd RCT for action during WWII." One of those Medal of Honor winners was a twenty-year-old from Hawaii, Daniel Inouye, who lost an arm fighting in Italy and so had to give up his dream of becoming a surgeon. Instead, he went on to be elected to the United States Senate, where he served for almost fifty years.

CHAPTER 25

FOUR WHO REFUSED

ALTHOUGH MOST JAPANESE PEOPLE were willing to endure both indignity and hardship to prove their patriotism, some refused. Among them were four who would eventually force the Supreme Court of the United States to rule on whether Congress and the president had violated the United States Constitution by imprisoning without trial American citizens who had never been accused of even the most trivial misdemeanor. Two would intentionally violate the dictates of Executive Order 9066 specifically to force such a court decision, the third would sue to regain employment, and the fourth would stay behind simply in order to remain with his girlfriend.

Gordon Hirabayashi was born in Washington State to Christian Issei parents whose flower farm had been seized under restrictive land laws. After high school, he enrolled at the University of Washington, and in the summer of 1940, he attended a YMCA leadership conference at Columbia

Gordon Hirabayashi.

University in New York, during which he became a pacifist. When he returned home, Hirabayashi joined the Quakers and registered as a conscientious objector. After a curfew was declared for anyone of Japanese ancestry, Hirabayashi decided to resist, continuing to move about freely as a law-abiding citizen. Instead of registering for relocation, Hirabayashi turned himself in to the FBI with the intention of creating a test case of the government's right to incarcerate Japanese Americans without due process of law.

Minoru "Min" Yasui, the son of two fruit pickers, was born in Oregon in 1916, and at the age of twenty-three had graduated from law school. At the time of Pearl Harbor, Yasui, who had been in ROTC, was a lieutenant in the army reserves. He tried to enlist in the regular army nine times, but his application was rejected. Yasui, the only attorney of Japanese heritage in Oregon, then opened a law practice to help with the Japanese community's legal needs.

On March 28, 1942, Yasui walked through downtown Portland after 8:00 p.m., deliberately violating the curfew. When a police officer refused to arrest him, he marched into the police station and demanded to be arrested there. The officer on duty did so.

Mitsuye Endo was the only woman among the four resisters. She went to secretarial school after high school in Sacramento and was then hired for a clerical job by the California Department of Motor Vehicles. Her employment included a

Minoru Yasui.

Fred T. Korematsu.

background check, which revealed she was Methodist, had a brother in the army, had never been to Japan, and was totally loyal to the United States. In the weeks after Pearl Harbor, however, she was fired from her job.

Fred Toyosaburo Korematsu was born in Oakland, California, on January 30, 1919, to parents who ran a flower nursery. After graduating from high school, he worked as a shipyard welder until, like Mitsuye Endo, he lost his job after Pearl Harbor. When the order for relocation came, Korematsu ignored it, unwilling to leave his Italian American girlfriend. He was arrested in May 1942. While awaiting trial, he was visited in jail by an attorney with the California branch of the American Civil Liberties Union. The California ACLU was looking for someone for whom it could file suit to test the constitutionality of Executive Order 9066.

Korematsu agreed and thus became the named plaintiff in one of the most important civil rights cases in American history. The California ACLU would file for Min Yasui and Gordon Hirabayashi as well, although neither of their cases would attain the notoriety of Fred Korematsu, the man who violated Executive Order 9066, because he was an American citizen.

From the first, the treatment of the four resisters bore little resemblance to the judicial process that most Americans believed was based on fairness and justice. Gordon Hirabayashi was held without bail for five months, until, at his trial, a jury found him guilty after deliberating for all of ten minutes. Min Yasui was convicted by a federal judge and sentenced to a year in prison and a $5,000 fine, the maximum under the law. Yasui was then held in solitary confinement in the county jail for nine months, denied exercise periods, showers, and a haircut. Fred Korematsu was also quickly found guilty and sent to the concentration camp in Topaz, Utah. Later, he would say, "I didn't feel guilty because I didn't do anything wrong . . . Every day in school, we said the pledge to the flag, 'with liberty and justice for all,' and I believed all that. I was an American citizen, and I had as many rights as anyone else."

All three resisters appealed their convictions, but in early 1943, a circuit court in San Francisco declined to rule and passed the cases to the United States Supreme Court. The Court heard the *Hirabayashi* and *Yasui* cases quickly, in May 1943. The issue in those lawsuits was narrow, whether or not the government had the right to impose a curfew, and did not deal with the broader question of internment. The specific question was "whether, acting in cooperation, Congress and the Executive have constitutional authority to impose the curfew . . . and whether the order itself was an appropriate means of carrying out the Executive Order for the 'protection against espionage and against sabotage.'"

The following month, by a unanimous vote, the Court ruled that the curfew was reasonable and upheld both convictions.

The power to wage war, Chief Justice Harlan Fiske Stone wrote, "extends to every matter and activity so related to war as substantially to affect its conduct and progress. The power is not restricted to the winning of victories in the field and the repulse of enemy forces. It embraces every phase of the national defense, including the protection of war materials and the members of the armed forces from injury and from the dangers which attend the rise, prosecution and progress of war."

And so, he concluded, because Japanese Americans had been largely shunned by whites, which "tended to increase their isolation, and in many instances their attachments to Japan and its institutions," the government was within its rights to deem them a threat, even those who were American citizens. In other words, Japanese Americans were allowed to be discriminated against because they had previously been discriminated against.

But the Court's ruling, as Justice Owen Roberts would put it, applied only to "a case of keeping people off the streets at night." The more significant question of whether forced relocation was permissible under the Constitution would wait for Fred Korematsu.

Although Korematsu's appeal had been heard in circuit

Hugo L. Black.

court at the same time as Yasui's and Hirabayashi's, it took an additional year for the Supreme Court to schedule the case. The decision, as in the previous cases, was for the government, although three justices issued stinging dissents.

The majority opinion, by Justice Hugo Black, a Ku Klux Klan member as a young man who became one of the nation's leading civil libertarians, began with a lofty statement of principles. "All legal restrictions which curtail the civil rights of a single racial group are immediately suspect. That is not to say that all such restrictions are unconstitutional. It is to say that courts must subject them to the most rigid scrutiny. Pressing public necessity may sometimes justify the existence of such restrictions; racial antagonism never can." From there, he proceeded to postulate pressing public necessity where none existed and deny the racial antagonism that was there for all to see.

"We are not unmindful of the hardships imposed by [the order] upon a large group of American citizens. But hardships are part of war, and war is an aggregation of hardships. All citizens alike, both in and out of uniform, feel the impact of war in greater or lesser measure. Citizenship has its responsibilities, as well as its privileges, and, in time of war, the burden is always heavier. Compulsory exclusion of large groups of citizens from their homes, except under circumstances of direst emergency and peril, is inconsistent with our basic governmental institutions. But when, under conditions of modern warfare, our shores are threatened by hostile forces, the power to protect must be commensurate with the threatened danger."

Justices Roberts, Jackson, and Murphy dissented. Jackson, who would later serve as the lead prosecutor at the Nuremburg war crimes trial, insisted that in upholding Fred Korematsu's conviction, "the Court for all time has validated the principle of racial discrimination in criminal procedure and of transplanting American citizens. The principle then lies about like a loaded weapon, ready for the hand of any authority that can bring forward a plausible claim of an urgent need. Every repetition imbeds that principle more deeply in our law and thinking and expands it to new purposes." Jackson's words ring as strongly now as they did then.

Mitsuye Endo is the least well-known of the four resisters, although she has a distinction the others lack. She won.

But her victory did not come without hardship. After Endo agreed to join in a lawsuit contesting whether "loyal Americans" could be deprived employment, she was sent to Tule Lake. She said later, "I agreed to do it at that moment,

Mitsuye Endo.

because they said it's for the good of everybody, and so I said, 'Well if that's it, I'll go ahead and do it.'"

Unlike in the cases of the three other resisters, Endo had not violated any of the rules set up by General DeWitt to enforce Executive Order 9066. As the war went on, with Japanese American soldiers amassing an extraordinary record in Italy, justice department lawyers began to become anxious about Endo's case. Government officials offered to release her from confinement as a way to end her lawsuit. But Endo refused and remained in the camp.

Her case, *Ex parte Endo*, was decided by the Supreme Court on December 18, 1944, the same day as *Korematsu*. Reversing its earlier position, in a unanimous decision, the Court ruled that "citizens who are concededly loyal" could not be held in War Relocation Authority concentration camps. Although the opinion, written by William O. Douglas, claimed that the Endo case was different because Endo had been investigated and proved loyal, he did not address how more than 100,000 Japanese Americans had been demonstrated to be even potentially disloyal. In addition, many former government and private employees who had undergone background checks had been incarcerated in the camps, Min Yasui, an army reservist, being a prominent example. In fact, it is difficult as a matter of law to see why the fundamental circumstances of *Endo* and *Korematsu* were at all different.

By December 1944, that Japan would lose the war seemed

certain, and officials in Washington were growing just a bit squeamish about their treatment of the Japanese. John DeWitt had been transferred to command the Army-Navy war college. (He would be promoted to full general by an act of Congress in 1954.) With DeWitt gone, a number of detainees had already been released, most taking work away from the West Coast, but some were allowed to return to their homes. Although the *Endo* ruling was narrow, to say nothing of face saving, many other internees were suddenly judged as "concededly loyal" and released.

Within months, the camps were closed.

EPILOGUE

SHAME

BY THE TIME WORLD War II ended on September 2, 1945, almost all of those whom the Supreme Court had deemed legally imprisoned had been freed to return to the West Coast and attempt to piece together their shattered lives. A few would find that their homes and property had been protected by sympathetic white residents, but for most, it meant virtually starting over, as if they were once again immigrants entering a foreign country. Records of their ownership of homes, property, and businesses had been largely destroyed, so most were unable to press claims for compensation.

Gordon Hirabayashi eventually earned a PhD in sociology at the University of Washington and taught both in the Middle East and Canada. For five years, he was chair of the sociology department at the University of Alberta. In 1987, the Ninth Circuit Court of Appeals set aside his conviction. There is a kiosk named for him in the Coronado National Forest, near the site of the prison in which he was held. Gordon Hirabayashi died on January 2, 2012, at age ninety-three, and that May, President Obama posthumously awarded him the Presidential Medal of Freedom, America's highest civilian honor.

After Min Yasui was released, "he took the Colorado bar exam in 1945 and had the highest scores of all the candidates. However, he was denied admission to the state's bar because of his wartime criminal record. He appealed to the state supreme court and won that case; he was admitted to the Colorado bar in January of 1946."

Yasui opened a law practice in Denver and spent the rest of his life fighting discrimination and injustice. He represented other Japanese Americans, often without fee but "also fought discrimination beyond the Japanese community. He was a founding member of the Urban League of Denver, an African American organization, in 1946, and helped found the Latin American Research and Service Agency (a Hispanic civil rights organization) and Denver Native Americans United."

Unlike Gordon Hirabayashi's, Yasui's conviction was not set aside in his lifetime. His appeal was pending when he died in 1986, and only afterward was his record cleared. He, too, was awarded the Presidential Medal of Freedom posthumously by President Obama.

Fred Korematsu, the only one of the four resisters without a political motive, was released from internment and worked as a welder in Salt Lake City and then as a draftsman in Detroit. His conviction, which had prevented him from getting a good job, was set aside in 1983. Like Min Yasui, Korematsu became a crusader against discrimination in all forms. After 9/11, he filed a "friend of the court" brief with the Supreme Court in support of those detained at Guantánamo Bay. In 1999, Korematsu was the only resister to be awarded the Medal of Freedom while still alive. He died six years later, at age eighty-six.

Mitsuye Endo was released shortly after the ruling in her favor and in 1946 married Kenneth Tsutsumi, whom she had met in the camps. They moved to Chicago, where they lived in a neighborhood favored by other Japanese families, and there raised their three children. Endo lived such an unassuming life that her daughter was in her twenties before she learned of her mother's role in ending internment.

Earl Warren was elected governor of California and then, in 1953, was named by President Eisenhower to be chief justice of the Supreme Court. One of the first cases he would hear was *Brown v. Board of Education*, which sought to declare segregation in public schools unconstitutional. For Warren, it was a chance at redemption. As he wrote later, he "deeply regretted the removal order and my own testimony advocating it, because it was not in keeping with our American concept of freedom and the rights of citizens . . .Whenever I thought of the innocent little children who were torn from home, school friends, and congenial surroundings, I was conscience-stricken . . . It was wrong to react so impulsively, without positive evidence of disloyalty."

The new chief justice navigated his way through many obstacles and obtained a 9–0 decision that proclaimed school segregation was wrong. But it was too late for the more than 100,000 innocent men, women, and children for whom Warren had decreed that segregation was right.

The scars, inflicted by some and borne by many, would last generations. Eventually, the government would make feeble attempts to right the terrible wrong. In 1952, a new immigration law finally guaranteed the right of Japanese immigrants to become naturalized citizens. In 1988, reparations of $20,000 per person were granted to surviving internees, a cheap price to pay to attempt to right a grievous wrong.

What is vital to appreciate is that neither the *Korematsu* decision nor the appalling violations of basic rights wrought by internment were created in a vacuum. Both were inevitable byproducts of a nation that had spent a century either perpetuating or acquiescing to slander and bigotry. Harlan Fiske Stone, Hugo Black, Earl Warren, and John DeWitt were no more responsible for the injustices perpetrated in the 1940s than were Horace Page, Ulysses Webb, James Phelan, Samuel Gompers, V. S. McClatchy, and William Randolph Hearst. Bigotry cannot be turned on and off like a water faucet. True democracy requires a constant commitment to not only safeguard the rights of those who cannot safeguard themselves but also not to tolerate those who would oppress the weak either through ignorance or for personal gain. Those who stand by and allow evil to be perpetrated when they are capable of doing something to stop it are as culpable as those who perpetrate it themselves.

And so, it would be sad enough if Japanese internment could be dismissed as an aberration of the American past, but the feelings and reasonings that resulted in that injustice are all too present in the nation today. On December 7, 2015, the seventy-fourth anniversary of the Japanese attack on Pearl Harbor, the *Washington Post* reported, "Donald Trump called Monday for a 'total and complete shutdown' of the entry of Muslims to the United States 'until our country's representatives can figure out what is going on.'" After his election, President Trump attempted to institute just such a ban. For a time, district and circuit courts, the lower two rungs on the federal judiciary ladder, ruled against the Trump administration, calling the proposal racially motivated, but eventually, after transparently sanitizing the initiative by restricting the order to citizens of specific countries that Trump claimed, without evidence, were hotbeds of terrorism, the Supreme Court in *Hawaii v. Trump* upheld the ban, as in *Korematsu*, on the grounds of national security.

To create some distance between his opinion and Justice Black's, Chief Justice Roberts, in his majority opinion in

Hawaii v. Trump, made a point of stating, "*Korematsu* has nothing to do with this case," because, he claimed, *Korematsu* was openly racist, where his opinion was based on national security grounds. Roberts seemed to miss the irony of the Supreme Court not officially admitting its error in *Korematsu* until it ruled that the government had the right to prevent Muslims from entering the United States. Under those circumstances, none of the four resisters would have applauded.

The chief justice also seemed unaware of what the two opinions actually said—or perhaps he was simply being disingenuous. As one legal scholar noted, "In a manner very much akin to Roberts's opinion in *Trump v. Hawaii*, Justice Hugo Black's opinion for the Court in *Korematsu* danced around and downplayed the openly racist context from which the government's exclusion order emerged."

Banning visitors on the basis of religion is not the only parallel with the imprisonment of Japanese Americans. The Trump administration also launched what can only be called a war against immigrants and asylum seekers from parts of the world that are home to nonwhites. "The country is full," he declared in April 2019 on Fox News. Those who do make it across the border are often shoved into camps built on the same principles as those that housed the Japanese. And, of course, Donald Trump made building a wall to separate the United States and Latin America one of the cornerstones of his presidency. Here again, the same five justices who allowed for the restriction of Muslims into the United States chose to ignore racist intent and allowed the Trump administration to divert funds allocated for military projects, including improved housing for soldiers in uniform, to be used to build the barrier.

Alexander Hamilton's insistence in *Federalist* 78 that the judiciary would be the "people's" branch of government, there to protect the weak against injustices that might be perpetrated by the legislative or the executive, has been cited countless times by scholars on the left and the right as a profound statement of American democratic principles. With Japanese Americans, first in 1922, and finally and most acutely during the 1940s, the judiciary instead betrayed those principles. For Japanese Americans, as with other groups deemed not white enough, democracy failed.

All Americans need to be aware of that failure if it is not to happen again.

BIBLIOGRAPHY

ONLINE RESOURCES

American Constitution Society. https://www.acslaw.org/expertforum/trump-v
-hawaii-and-chief-justice-robertss-korematsu-overruled-parlor-trick/.

Chinese Historical Society of America. https://www.chsa.org/wp-content/uploads
/2013/04/Relocation.pdf.

Densho Encyclopedia. http://encyclopedia.densho.org.

Digital History. https://www.digitalhistory.uh.edu/active_learning/explorations
/japanese_internment/munson_report.cfm.

Digital Public Library of America. https://dp.la/exhibitions/japanese-internment
/home-family/.

Eccentric Culinary History. https://eccentricculinary.com/the-great-sushi-craze
-of-1905-part-1/.

FindLaw. https://blogs.findlaw.com/supreme_court/2015/10/13-worst-supreme
-court-decisions-of-all-time.html.

Google Arts and Culture. https://artsandculture.google.com/exhibit/earthquake-the
-chinatown-story-chinese-historical-society-of-america/gQr-sWsc?hl=en.

Library of Congress Classroom Materials. https://www.loc.gov/classroom-materials
/immigration/japanese/behind-the-wire.

Literary Hub. https://lithub.com/the-forgotten-internment-of-japanese-americans
-in-hawaii/.

Newspapers.com.

NPR.org. https://www.npr.org/templates/story/story.php?storyId=5337215.

Northeast Museum Services Center. https://nmscarcheologylab.wordpress.com
/2014/03/18/a-tale-of-two-nations-victorian-america-and-the-japan-craze/.

San Francisco State University Collections. https://diva.sfsu.edu/collections/ga1907
/bundles/216052.

Time. https://time.com/5802127/hawaii-internment-order/.

Wikimedia. https://commons.wikimedia.org/wiki/File:No_Japs_in_Our_Schools.jpg.

REFERENCE MATERIAL

—Annals of the Congress of the United States.

—*The American Journal of International Law*, Vol. 5, No. 2, Supplement: Official Documents.

—*Congressional Globe.*

—*Congressional Record.*

—Documental history of law cases affecting Japanese in the United States. Privately printed, 1925.

—Records and Briefs of the United States Supreme Court.

—Statutes at Large.

—United States Reports.

BOOKS AND ARTICLES

"The California Alien Land Law." *Southern Bench and Bar Review*, Vol. 1, No. 4 (July 1913).

Allerfeldt, Kristofer. "Race and Restriction: Anti-Asian Immigration Pressures in the Pacific North-west of America during the Progressive Era, 1885–1924." *History*, Vol. 88 (January 2003).

Aoki, Keith. "No Right to Own?: The Early Twentieth Century 'Alien Land Laws' as a Prelude to Internment." *Boston College Third World Law Journal*, Vol. 19 (December 1998).

Bailey, Thomas. "California, Japan, and the Alien Land Legislation of 1913." *Pacific Historical Review*, Vol. 1, No. 1 (March 1932).

Berger, Bethany R. "Birthright Citizenship on Trial: Elk v. Wilkins and United States v. Wong Kim Ark." *Cardozo Law Review*, Vol. 37, No. 4 (April 2016).

Bowling, Kenneth R., and Helen E. Veit (eds). *The Diary of William Maclay and Other Notes on Senate Debates*. Baltimore, MD: Johns Hopkins University Press, 1988.

Brudnoy, David. "Race and the San Francisco School Board Incident: Contemporary Evaluations." *California Historical Quarterly*, Vol. 50, No. 3 (September 1971).

Buell, Raymond L. "The Development of the Anti-Japanese Agitation in the United States." *Political Science Quarterly*, Vol. 37, No. 4 (December 1922).

Carbado, Devon. "Yellow by Law." *California Law Review*, Vol. 97, No. 3 (June 2009).

Castleman, Bruce. "California's Alien Land Laws." *Western Legal History*, Vol. 7, No. 25 (Winter/Spring 1994).

Chambers, John S. "The Japanese Invasion." *The Annals of the American Academy of Political and Social Science*, Vol. 93, No. 1 (January 1921).

Cho, Sumi. "Redeeming Whiteness in the Shadow of Internment: Earl Warren, Brown, and a Theory of Racial Redemption." *Boston College Third World Law Journal*, Vol. 19, No. 1 (December 1998).

Collins, Charles Wallace. "Will the California Alien Land Law Stand the Test of the Fourteenth Amendment?" *Yale Law Journal*, Vol. 23, No. 4 (February 1914).

Conmy, Peter T. "The History of California's Japanese Problem and the Part Played by the Native Sons of the Golden West in its Solution." Privately printed, 1942.

Coulson, Doug. "British Imperialism, the Indian Independence Movement, and the Racial Eligibility Provisions of the Naturalization Act: *United States v. Thind* Revisited." *Georgetown Journal of Law & Modern Critical Race Perspectives*, Vol. 7 (2015).

Cray, Ed. *Chief Justice: A Biography of Earl Warren*, New York: Simon & Schuster, 1997.

Daniels, Roger. *The Politics of Prejudice: The Anti-Japanese Movement in California and the Struggle for Japanese Exclusion*. Berkeley: University of California Press, 1977.

Ferguson, Edwin E. "The California Alien Land Law and the Fourteenth Amendment." *California Law Review*, Vol. 35 (March 1947).

Goto, Baron Shimpei. "The Anti-Japanese Question in California." *The Annals of the American Academy of Political and Social Science*, Vol. 93 (January 1921).

Gripentrog, John. "The Transnational Pastime: Baseball and American Perceptions of Japan in the 1930s." *Diplomatic History*, Vol. 34, No. 2 (April 2010).

Hajimu, Masuda. "Rumors of War: Immigration Disputes and the Social Construction of American-Japanese Relations, 1905–1913." *Diplomatic History*, Vol. 33, No. 1 (January 2009).

Haney López, Ian. *White by Law: The Legal Construction of Race*. New York: New York University Press, 2006.

Hichborn, Franklin. *Story of the Session of the California Legislature of 1913*. San Francisco: Press of the James H. Barry Company, 1913.

Ichioka, Yuji. "Amerika Nadeshiko: Japanese Immigrant Women in the United States, 1900–1924." *Pacific Historical Review*, Vol. 49, No. 2 (May 1980).

———. "Japanese Immigrant Response to the 1920 California Alien Land Law." *Agricultural History*, Vol. 58, No. 2 (April 1984).

Inui, Kiyo Sue. "The Gentlemen's Agreement. How It Has Functioned." *The Annals of the American Academy of Political and Social Science*, Vol. 122 (November 1925).

Iwata, Masakazu. "The Japanese Immigrants in California Agriculture." *Agricultural History*, Vol. 36, No. 1 (January 1962).

Kanzaki, Kiichi. "Is the Japanese Menace in America a Reality?" *The Annals of the American Academy of Political and Social Science*, Vol. 93 (January 1921).

Kennan, George. "The Fight for Reform in San Francisco." *McClure's Magazine*, September 1907.

Le Pore, Herbert P. "Prelude to Prejudice: Hiram Johnson, Woodrow Wilson, and the California Alien Land Law Controversy of 1913." *Southern California Quarterly*, Vol. 61, No. 1 (Spring 1979).

Loureiro, Pedro A. "Japanese Espionage and American Countermeasures in Pre-Pearl Harbor California." *Journal of American-East Asian Relations*, Vol. 3, No. 3 (Fall 1994).

Manzella, Abigail G. H. *Migrating Fictions: Gender, Race, and Citizenship in U.S. Internal Displacements*. Columbus: The Ohio State University Press, 2018.

Muller, Eric. *American Inquisition. The Hunt for Japanese American Disloyalty in World War II*. Chapel Hill: University of North Carolina Press, 2007.

Older, Mrs. Fremont. *San Francisco: The Magic City*. New York: Longmans, Green, 1961.

Page, Thomas Walker. "The San Francisco Labor Movement in 1901." *Political Science Quarterly*, Vol. 17, No. 4 (December 1902).

Peffer, George Anthony. "Forbidden Families: Emigration Experiences of Chinese Women Under the Page Law, 1875–1882." *Journal of American Ethnic History*, Vol. 6, No. 1 (Fall 1986).

Phelan, James D. "Why California Objects to the Japanese Invasion." *The Annals of the American Academy of Political and Social Science*, Vol. 93, No. 1 (January 1921).

Rast, Raymond W. "The Cultural Politics of Tourism in San Francisco's Chinatown, 1882–1917." *Pacific Historical Review*, Vol. 76, No. 1 (February 2007).

Roodner, Theodore. "Washington's Alien Land Law—Its Constitutionality." *Washington Law Review*, Vol. 39, No. 1 (Spring 1964).

Startt, James D. *Woodrow Wilson and the Press: Prelude to the Presidency*. New York: Palgrave Macmillan, 2004.

Tygiel, Jules. ". . . Where Unionism Holds Undisputed Sway.: A Reappraisal of San Francisco's Union Labor Party." *California History*, Vol. 62, No. 3 (Fall 1983).

Williams, C. C. "Congressional Career of the Hon. H. F. Page, Representative of the Second District of California and Renominated for a Fifth Term." San Francisco: Francis, Valentine, printers, 1880.

Wilson, Woodrow. *A History of the American People. Volume Five*. New York: Harper and Brothers, 1903.

SOURCE NOTES

PROLOGUE

Korematsu was listed as the third worst decision ever . . . https://blogs.findlaw.com
/supreme_court/2015/10/13-worst-supreme-court-decisions-of-all-time.html.

"live very plainly and work . . ." Goto, Baron Shimpei. "The Anti-Japanese Question in
California." *The Annals of the American Academy of Political and Social Science*, Vol.
93, No. 1 (January 1921), p. 104.

"we admire their industry and cleverness . . ." "The people of Asia . . ." "We are willing to
receive diplomats . . ." Phelan, James D. "Why California Objects to the Japanese
Invasion." Ibid., p. 17.

"Assimilation is impossible . . ." "Watch the gopher at work . . ." Chambers, John S.
"The Japanese Invasion." Ibid., pp. 24–5.

"An official report noted that by 1910 . . ." Allerfeldt, Kristofer. "Race and Restriction:
Anti-Asian Immigration Pressures in the Pacific North-west of America during the
Progressive Era, 1885–1924." *History*, Vol. 88 (January 2003), p. 54.

CHAPTER 1: FREE AND WHITE

"Indians who don't pay taxes." *Annals of the Congress of the United States*, Vol. 1,
p. 1111.

"The reason of admitting foreigners . . ." Ibid.

"When we are considering the advantages . . ." Ibid.

"That any alien, being a free white person . . ." 1 Statutes at Large 103.

"The truth of the matter is that it is a Vile bill . . ." Bowling, Kenneth R., and Helen E.
Veit (eds), *The Diary of William Maclay and Other Notes on Senate Debates* (Baltimore,
MD: Johns Hopkins University Press, 1988), p. 208.

"[a] negro of the African race . . ." 60 U.S. 393.

"had for more than a century before been regarded . . ." Ibid.

CHAPTER 2: WHITE, BLACK, . . . AND GOLD

"I content myself for the present . . ." *Congressional Globe*, Third Session, 40th
Congress, Part 2, p. 1034.

"I am in favor of the position of the Senator from Massachusetts . . ." Ibid., p. 1036.

"never intended that Chinese . . ." *Journal of the House of Representatives*, March 4, 1860.

"I hope a large majority of the good people of this country . . ." "How can any lover of
this country ask for free Chinese immigration . . ." *Congressional Globe*, Second
Session, 41st Congress, Part 1, p. 756.

"end the danger of cheap Chinese labor . . ." Peffer, George Anthony. "Forbidden
Families: Emigration Experiences of Chinese Women Under the Page Law,
1875–1882." *Journal of American Ethnic History*, Vol. 6, No. 1 (Fall 1986), p. 28.

"Ever mindful of the Asiatic curse resting upon California . . ." "check or altogether prevent Chinese immigration . . ." Williams, C. C. "Congressional Career of the Hon. H. F. Page, Representative of the Second District of California and Renominated for a Fifth Term." (San Francisco: Francis, Valentine & Co., printers, 1880), p. 10.

"place a dividing line . . ." "send the brazen harlot . . ." "with their wives and children . . ." "deadly blight." Appendix to the *Congressional Record*, 43rd Congress, Second Session, Vol. 3, p. 44.

CHAPTER 3: AH YUP

"For the first time in the history of the city of New York . . ." *New York Herald*, November 28, 1878, p. 5.

"The moment you appear at the ballot box . . ." Berger, Bethany R. "Birthright Citizenship on Trial: Elk v. Wilkins and United States v. Wong Kim Ark." *Cardozo Law Review*, Vol. 37, No. 4 (April 2016), p. 1220.

"Those called white may be found in every shade . . ." "as ordinarily used everywhere . . ." 5 Sawyer 155; 6 Central Law Journal 387 (1878).

"A Mongolian is not . . ." Ibid.

"There has hardly been a session of Congress . . ." Williams, p. 3.

CHAPTER 4: ENTER THE JAPANESE

"Over the next twenty years . . ." https://nmscarcheologylab.wordpress .com/2014/03/18/a-tale-of-two-nations-victorian-america-and-the-japan-craze/.

"My visit to Japan . . ." https://eccentricculinary.com/the-great-sushi-craze-of-1905 -part-1/.

"The American interest in Japan created a booming export market . . ." https:// nmscarcheologylab.wordpress.com/2014/03/18/a-tale-of-two-nations-victorian -america-and-the-japan-craze/.

"White workers, including ignorant ones . . ." Carbado, Devon. "Yellow by Law." *California Law Review*, Vol. 97, No. 3 (June 2009), p. 641.

CHAPTER 5: BIRTHRIGHT

The following year, that number was increased . . . Although Wong Kim Ark's birth year is generally given as 1873, the only document that contains that date is his habeas corpus petition. Most other documents, including his immigration form, list the year as 1871, which, given the later timeline, is more likely.

He visited them in 1890 and returned to the United States . . . Wong's travels are detailed in Berger, Bethany R. "Birthright Citizenship on Trial: Elk v. Wilkins and United States v. Wong Kim Ark." *Cardozo Law Review*, Vol. 37, No. 4 (April 2016), p. 1185–1258.

"If this young Chinaman should be declared to be a citizen . . ." Ibid.

"claimed that Chinese could not . . ." January 4, 1896, p. 3.

"Chinese born in this country . . . are citizens of the United States . . ." *Sacramento Daily Union*, January 4, 1896, p. 3.

"They will be, at least and by all means, examined most severely . . ." *San Francisco Call*, January 4, 1896, p. 5.

"born in the United States, of parents of Chinese descent . . ." 169 U.S. 649.

"To hold that the Fourteenth Amendment of the Constitution excludes . . ." Ibid.

CHAPTER 6: EXCLUSION

"financed California playwrights, artists, and sculptors . . ." Older, Mrs. Fremont. *San Francisco: The Magic City* (New York: Longmans, Green, 1961), p. 187.

"to rid the city of the domination of bosses." Ibid., p. 78.

"the waste and extravagance . . ." "municipal offices are conducted" *San Francisco Call*, November 7, 1896, p. 9.

"There is not bubonic plague in San Francisco . . ." "a bold attempt to blackmail . . ." *San Francisco Call*, March 8, 1900, p. 3.

"enthusiastic and largely attended mass meeting . . ." "to protest the violations . . ." Details of the meeting from *San Francisco Call*, May 8, 1900, p. 12.

"The Chinese and Japanese were impossible among us . . ." "It would be better . . ." Ibid.

"the adoption of an act of Congress . . ." Ibid.

"the assumed virtue of the Japanese, i.e., *their partial adoption of American customs* . . ." Ibid. Italics added.

"devoted to raising all of the standards . . ." Kanzaki, Kiichi. "Is the Japanese Menace in America a Reality?" *The Annals of the American Academy of Political and Social Science*, Vol. 93 (January 1921), pp. 88–97.

The Japanese government, hoping to keep America as an ally . . . Japanese immigration was more than halved the following year, dropping from more than twelve thousand to just less than five thousand.

CHAPTER 7: THE WORKERS . . .

"check the growing evils . . ." Page, Thomas Walker. "The San Francisco Labor Movement in 1901." *Political Science Quarterly*, Vol. 17, No. 4 (December 1902), p. 668.

The following night, a patrolman found himself . . . *San Francisco Examiner*, July 26, 1901, p. 3.

"We have things just . . ." Page, p. 679.

"Vessels were deserted by their sailors . . ." Ibid.

CHAPTER 8: . . . AND THE BOSS

"designed to gain the support of workingmen . . ." Tygiel, Jules. ". . .Where Unionism Holds Undisputed Sway.: A Reappraisal of San Francisco's Union Labor Party." *California History*, Vol. 62, No. 3 (Fall 1983), p. 203.

"Kearny Street between Market and Post streets . . ." *San Francisco Call*, September 30, 1901, p. 5.

"People Rebuke Bosses" *San Francisco Call*, November 6, 1901, p. 1.

"I regard my election as a just and overwhelming rebuke . . ." Ibid.

"the administration made a business of selling . . ." Kennan, George. "The Fight for Reform in San Francisco." *McClure's Magazine*, September 1907, p. 547.

"Skilled workmen who before the election of Mayor Schmitz . . ." "I don't care how much they steal . . ." Ibid.

"the character and rapidly increasing numbers of Japanese . . ." Buell, Raymond L. "The Development of the Anti-Japanese Agitation in the United States." *Political Science Quarterly*, Vol. 37, No. 4 (December 1922), p. 609.

CHAPTER 9: TREMORS

"Earthquake and Fire: San Francisco in Ruins." *Call-Chronicle-Examiner*, April 19, 1906, p. 1.

"After darkness, thousands of the homeless . . ." Ibid.

"Everybody in San Francisco is prepared to leave the city . . ." Ibid.

"The cities in the immediate vicinity of San Francisco bay . . ." "Let Us Have No More Chinatowns in Our Cities." *Oakland Enquirer*, April 23, 1906. https://artsandculture .google.com/exhibit/earthquake-the-chinatown-story-chinese-historical-society -of-america/gQr-sWsc?hl=en.

"prime real estate . . . with commanding views." https://www.npr.org/templates/story /story.php?storyId=5337215.

"China at present is one of the greatest markets . . ." "It would not be best to San Francisco's interests . . ." *Oakland Tribune*, May 10, 1906, p. 4

"implemented by we Chinese quickly, or we will soon regret it." . . . "[h]ire famous attorneys to represent us as soon as possible . . ." "Western landlords like to rent their houses . . ." https://www.chsa.org/wp-content/uploads/2013/04/Relocation.pdf.

"distinguished by pagoda-like towers . . ." Rast, Raymond W. "The Cultural Politics of Tourism in San Francisco's Chinatown, 1882–1917." *Pacific Historical Review*, Vol. 76, No. 1 (February 2007), pp. 53–4.

"Mayor Schmitz, the tool of Ruef . . ." *Spokane Press*, October 31, 1906, p. 4.

"In the municipal administration . . ." Inui, Kiyo Sue. "The Gentlemen's Agreement. How It Has Functioned." *The Annals of the American Academy of Political and Social Science*, Vol. 122 (November 1925), p. 189.

CHAPTER 10: A CONVENIENT TARGET

"the School Board of the city . . ." Ibid.

"Resolved that the Board of Education is determined . . ." Buell, p. 623.

"enabled Schmitz and Ruef . . ." Ibid.

"on July 23, 1906 . . ." Ibid.

As early as December 1905, William Randolph Hearst's *San Francisco Examiner* . . . Daniels, Roger. *The Politics of Prejudice: The Anti-Japanese Movement in California and the Struggle for Japanese Exclusion* (Berkeley: University of California Press, 1977), p. 70.

Finally, there were less than 3,000 Japanese people in San Francisco . . . Japanese population in 1900 was 1,781, which grew to 4,518 in 1910, but, as will be seen, there was a large-scale influx of Japanese women after 1907. https://www.sfgenealogy.org /sf/history/hgpop.htm.

"Stand up, Japanese nation! Our countrymen . . ." Hajimu, Masuda. "Rumors of War: Immigration Disputes and the Social Construction of American-Japanese Relations, 1905–1913." *Diplomatic History*, Vol. 33, No. 1 (January 2009), p. 11.

"I believe it possible . . ." docs.google.com/viewerng/viewer?url=https://diva.sfsu.edu
/bundles/preview/352014?token%3DL0ZkALVIjH.

"went into a rage, moved to sue . . ." Brudnoy, David. "Race and the San Francisco
School Board Incident: Contemporary Evaluations." *California Historical Quarterly*,
Vol. 50, No. 1 (September 1971), p. 297.

"The United States will not for a moment entertain . . ." Buell, p. 624.

"After my conversation with the President of the Board of Education . . ." https://diva
.sfsu.edu/collections/ga1907/bundles/215932.

"The Japanese immigrant is not an immigrant . . ." *Boston Globe*, December 2, 1906, p. 4.

"Japan Sounds Our Coasts . . ." *San Francisco Enquirer*, December 20, 1906, p. 1.

"The overwhelming mass of our people cherish . . ." http://encyclopedia.densho.org
/San_Francisco_school_segregation/.

"an effort on the part of the labor unions . . ." *San Francisco Call*, December 11, 1906, p. 7.

CHAPTER 11: MR. SCHMITZ GOES TO WASHINGTON

"We are going to get the crooks.": *San Francisco Call*, October 23, 1906, p. 1.

"With unparalleled audacity Abe Ruef ordered . . ." Ibid.

"With the fullest sense of the responsibility resting upon me . . ." Ibid.

"No Japs in Our Schools." https://commons.wikimedia.org/wiki/File:No_Japs_in
_Our_Schools.jpg.

"When Ruef and Schmitz were finally brought to trial . . ." Buell, p. 612.

"A letter just received from one of the shrewdest and most experienced observers I
know . . ." https://diva.sfsu.edu/collections/ga1907/bundles/216052.

"This may be all wrong— . . ." Ibid.

"The relations between the Mayor and the President . . ." *San Francisco Call*, February
4, 1907, p. 1.

"We have come here with open minds . . ." *San Francisco Call*, February 8, 1907, p 1.

"We will not stand on technicalities . . ." Ibid.

"received assurances that the immigration of Japanese laborers . . ." *New York Times*,
February 19, 1907, p. 5.

"'laborers who have already been in America . . ." Daniels, p. 44.

CHAPTER 12: HERE COME THE BRIDES

In 1909, when the program had fully taken effect . . . Inui, p. 193.

By 1910, the number of married women had increased . . . Ichioka, Yuji. "Amerika
Nadeshiko: Japanese Immigrant Women in the United States, 1900–1924." *Pacific
Historical Review*, Vol. 49, No. 2 (May 1980), p. 341.

"genuinely shocked to see their husbands . . ." Ibid., p. 347.

"At the turn of the century, there were only 269 children . . ." Ibid., p. 354.

"The growth of Nisei children accelerated . . ." Ibid., p. 355.

CHAPTER 13: THIS LAND IS (NOT) YOUR LAND

"Progressives in California believed that economic self-preservation . . ." Le Pore,
Herbert P. "Prelude to Prejudice: Hiram Johnson, Woodrow Wilson, and the

California Alien Land Law Controversy of 1913." *Southern California Quarterly*, Vol. 61, No. 1 (Spring 1979), p. 100.

"municipal segregation ordinance . . ." Ibid., p. 47.

"Had California been an independent republic . . ." Ibid., p. 46.

"those infernal fools . . ." "worse than the stupidity of the San Francisco mob . . ." Hajimu, p. 18.

"half a thousand of San Francisco's leading businessmen . . ." *San Francisco Call*, December 8, 1909, p. 1.

"destined even in its inception . . ." Ibid.

"full liberty to enter, travel, or reside . . ." "on equal terms" "rights of residence . . ." *New York Times*, July 27, 1939, p. 8.

"to carry on trade, wholesale and retail . . ." "to own or lease and occupy houses, manufactories, warehouses, and ships . . ." Ibid.

"The Japanese have invaded the central valleys of California . . ." Daniels, p. 55.

The Japanese represented only 2 percent of California's population and owned less than one-tenth of a percent of the state's land. Bailey, Thomas. "California, Japan, and the Alien Land Legislation of 1913." *Pacific Historical Review*, Vol. 1, No. 1 (March 1932), p. 38.

An additional .5 percent, or 80,000 acres, was leased from white owners. Iwata, Masakazu. "The Japanese Immigrants in California Agriculture." *Agricultural History*, Vol. 36, No. 1 (January 1962), p. 29.

CHAPTER 14: FAKE NEWS

"Hearst, as a college student who preferred pranks to studies . . ." Startt, James D. *Woodrow Wilson and the Press: Prelude to the Presidency* (New York: Palgrave Macmillan, 2004), p. 157.

"multitudes of men . . ." Wilson, Woodrow. *A History of the American People. Volume Five* (New York: Harper and Brothers, 1903), pp. 213–4.

"the Chinese were more to be desired . . ." Ibid.

"many an unsavory habit . . ." "it was their skill . . . " Ibid.

"Has governor spoken against . . ." Daniels, p. 55.

"In the matter of Chinese and Japanese Coolie immigration . . ." *The American Journal of International Law*, Vol. 5, No. 2, Supplement: Official Documents, April 1911, pp. 107–8.

"The fundamental question is not one of race discrimination . . ." 263 U.S. 225 (1923).

"a crowd of approximately 20,000 . . ." *San Francisco Examiner*, March 20, 1913, p. 1; Le Pore, p. 105.

With his eye on the United States Senate seat . . . With the Seventeenth Amendment, senators would no longer be appointed.

"aliens eligible for citizenship . . ." "aliens ineligible for citizenship . . ." Hichborn, Franklin. *Story of the Session of the California Legislature of 1913* (San Francisco: Press of the James H. Barry Company, 1913), p. 262.

"The fundamental basis of all legislation . . ." Ferguson, Edwin E. "The California Alien Land Law and the Fourteenth Amendment." *California Law Review*, Vol. 35 (March 1947), p. 68.

"warned the committee . . ." Hichborn, p. 243.

"It is contended that the classification of aliens . . ." "The California law will in all probability . . ." Collins, Charles Wallace. "Will the California Alien Land Law Stand the Test of the Fourteenth Amendment?" *Yale Law Journal*, Vol. 23, No. 4 (February 1914), pp. 333–8.

"The real danger [to the land law] lies in . . ." "The California Alien Land Law." *Southern Bench and Bar Review*, Vol. 1, No. 4 (July 1913), p. 253.

"one Akhay Kumar Mozumdar . . ." "first of his race." "a high-caste . . ." "always considered himself . . ." Ibid.

CHAPTER 15: SLAMMING THE GOLDEN DOOR

"Japanese farmers were able to place land in trusts . . ." Aoki, Keith. "No Right to Own?: The Early Twentieth-Century 'Alien Land Laws' as a Prelude to Internment." *Boston College Third World Law Journal*, Vol. 19 (December 1998), p. 56.

Rather than decrease . . . Ichioka, Yuji. "Japanese Immigrant Response to the 1920 California Alien Land Law." *Agricultural History*, Vol. 58, No. 2 (April 1984), p. 162.

"Japan's Plan to Invade and Conquer the United States . . ." "The Humiliating Terms of Peace . . ." *San Francisco Examiner*, October 10, 1915, pp. 26–7.

"idiots, imbeciles, epileptics . . ." Ibid.

"effective discipline exercised . . ." *New York Times*, January 17, 1917, p. 10.

"It is not a test of character . . ." Ibid.

"at the request of the State Department . . ." *New York Times*, February 6, 1917, p. 12.

CHAPTER 16: ALL IN THE FAMILY

"that he had no intention of doing anything but make a gift of the property . . ." Documental history of law cases affecting Japanese in the United States. Privately printed, 1925, p. 733.

"he had lost one child while living in a rooming house . . ." Ibid.

"every means to oust the Haradas from the community . . ." Castleman, Bruce. "California's Alien Land Laws." *Western Legal History*, Vol. 7, No. 25 (Winter/Spring 1994), p. 36.

"fifteen residents signed a petition . . ." Ibid.

"Jap children" Ibid.

"The question of whether a Japanese person is not eligible to citizenship . . ." "Natives of Japan are . . . classified as . . ." Documental history, p. 721.

"the Japanese counsel from Los Angeles . . ." *Sacramento Star*, December 29, 1916, p. 1.

"There is nothing to prevent the state of California from becoming Japanized!" Ibid.

"The argument of counsel for plaintiff . . ." Documental history, 733.

"If an embarrassing or unfortunate . . ." Ibid.

CHAPTER 17: THE GOLDEN WEST

"In the streets of Seoul . . ." *San Francisco Examiner*, April 3, 1919, p. 2.

"stories of brutality sustained" Ibid.

"Keep California White" *Sacramento Bee*, April 1, 1919, pp. 1, 9.

"During my investigations into the Japanese situation . . ." Ibid.

"Publicity is something they do not like . . ." Ibid.

"perhaps the most influential pressure group in the State." Daniels, p. 85.

"embracing only the sons of those sturdy pioneers . . ." *New York Times*, July 11, 1884, p. 3.

"as it has always been and . . ." *The Grizzly Bear*. Both groups still exist.

"Official Native Son interest in the problem began in 1907 . . ." Conmy, Peter T. "The History of California's Japanese Problem and the Part Played by the Native Sons of the Golden West in its Solution." Privately printed, 1942, p. 2.

"Would you like your daughter to marry a Japanese?" Daniels, p. 85.

"If not, demand your representatives . . ." Ibid.

"One of the factors which contributed greatly to the exclusion movement . . ." Ibid., p. 6.

"Japanese Exclusion League of California Formally Organized." *Sacramento Bee*, September 2, 1920, p.1.

"The body will seek passage of an Anti-Alien Land Act . . ." Ibid.

The Exclusion League published a five-point program . . . Daniels, p. 85. Similar proposals are popular among conservatives today.

"Having made an unavailing fight Tuesday to defeat . . ." *San Francisco Examiner*, November 4, 1920, p. 1.

CHAPTER 18: THE HEART OF AN AMERICAN

"scientific course." *Oakland Tribune*, June 3, 1903, p. 8.

He got married, had five children, got a clerical or sales job . . . His only son would die serving in the United States Army in World War II.

They instructed him to accept the application . . . *Honolulu Star Bulletin*, October 16, 1914, p. 4.

"underwent a lengthy examination by Judge Dole . . ." "samurai . . ." "I am pure Japanese . . ." "under the Stars and Stripes" *Honolulu Star Bulletin*, January 30, 1915, p. 1.

"Some of the scholars say that the Japanese are not Mongolians . . ." "He is all right, the only question being that he is a Japanese . . ." Ibid.

Ozawa, again representing himself, filed . . . Records and Briefs of the United States Supreme Court, Vol. 484, p. 987.

"There is not a special law prohibiting Japanese from naturalization . . ." Ibid.

"I neither drink liquor of any kind, nor smoke . . ." Quoted in Haney López, Ian. *White by Law: The Legal Construction of Race* (New York: New York University Press, 2006), pp. 56–7.

Ozawa made practical points as well . . . *Honolulu Star Bulletin*, June 9, 1915, p. 3.

"What will the United States gain by humiliating the Japanese . . ." *Honolulu Star Bulletin*, June 10, 1915, p. 2.

Thompson also filed a note stating Ozawa was morally unfit . . . *Honolulu Advertiser*, August 1, 1915, p. 14.

"It would give the able Japanese in Hawaii . . ." *Honolulu Star Bulletin*, March 24, 1916, p. 3.

"The remedy lies with Congress . . ." *Honolulu Star Bulletin*, March 25, 1916, pp. 1, 8.

His last sentence was either hopelessly naive . . . On the same day, Clemons ruled that two Filipino merchant seamen were eligible for citizenship because the Philippines was a protectorate of the United States.

Just five days later . . . *Honolulu Star Bulletin*, March 30, 1916, p. 2.

"discuss ways and means . . ." *Honolulu Advertiser*, August 7, 1916, p. 1.

One source of opposition to Ozawa's mounting an appeal . . . *Honolulu Star Bulletin*, December 19, 1917, p. 7.

Taft declined . . . *Honolulu Star Bulletin*, February 8, 1918, p. 2.

"The reason for the postponement . . ." "It is considered . . ." *Honolulu Star Bulletin*, March 27, 1919, p. 1.

"has traced the history of Japan . . ." *Buffalo (NY) Times*, August 9, 1922, p. 2.

"quiet little man . . ." "ruled his whole life . . ." A companion case was argued as well, *Yamashita v. Hinkle*, in which two Japanese immigrants who had been naturalized in Washington State prior to the 1906 law were denied the right to incorporate a real estate holding company, because the naturalizations were illegal, thus upholding Washington's alien land law.

"The provision is not that Negroes . . ." "It is not enough to say . . ." 260 U.S. 178 (1922).

"Color of the skin . . ." Ibid.

"in an almost unbroken line, have held . . ." Ibid.

In another decision, a federal judge ruled . . . 179 Fed. 1002 (1910).

"Controversies have arisen . . ." Ibid.

"is clearly of a race which is not Caucasian . . ." Ibid. The Court ruled against Yamashita as well, thus voiding all previous naturalizations of the Japanese.

"Of course, there is not implied . . ." Ibid.

"far toward checking the 'yellow peril' . . ." *San Francisco Examiner*, November 14, 1922, p. 1.

Both Ulysses Webb and James Phelan were overjoyed . . . *Sacramento Star*, November 13, 1922, p. 10.

"It is absurd, of course . . ." *Honolulu Star Bulletin*, November 15, 1922, p. 6.

"radical cure of this international ill . . ." Ibid.

"How hypocritical . . ." Ibid.

CHAPTER 19: WHAT MEETS THE EYE

his character described as "excellent." Records and Briefs of the United States Supreme Court, Vol. 484, p. 1072.

"The testimony in the case . . ." "an advocate of the principle of India . . ." Coulson, Doug. "British Imperialism, the Indian Independence Movement, and the Racial Eligibility Provisions of the Naturalization Act: *United States v. Thind* Revisited." *Georgetown Journal of Law & Modern Critical Race Perspectives*, Vol. 7 (2015), pp. 20–1.

"disinterested citizens, who . . ." Ibid.

"It must be concluded . . ." "that Bhagat Singh is entitled to naturalization." Records and Briefs of the United States Supreme Court, October Term 1922, Number 202, p. 3.

"little ground for challenge . . ." "the decision in Ozawa . . ." Ibid.

"It may be assumed . . ." "that the terms 'Caucasian' and 'white persons' are synonymous . . ." Ibid., pp. 8–9.

"The intention was to confer the privilege of citizenship . . ." 261 U.S. 204 (1923).

"The conclusion that the phrase . . ." "In the endeavor to . . ." Ibid.

"The children of English, . . ."

CHAPTER 20: TURNING THE SOIL

"the Japanese, through his skill and effort . . ." Roodner, Theodore. "Washington's
  Alien Land Law—Its Constitutionality." *Washington Law Review*, Vol. 39, No. 1
  (Spring 1964), p. 118.
"not include lands containing . . ." "the necessary land for mills . . ." "an alien who had
  not . . ." https://cite.case.law/f/274/841/.
"that the public welfare is directly affected . . ." "The most drastic action in this regard . . ."
  United States Reports: Cases Adjudged in the Supreme Court, Vol. 263, p. 207.
"In the field of agriculture, the American and Oriental cannot compete . . ." Ibid.
"Appellants' contention that the state act discriminates . . ." Ibid., p. 220.
"The Terraces, who are citizens . . ." 263 U.S. 197 (1923)
"a capable farmer," "substantially similar to that granted to a lessee." 263 U.S. 313 (1923).
"forbid indirect as well as direct ownership . . ." 263 US 326 (1923).

CHAPTER 21: BANZAI AND BASEBALL

"The report of the [A.F. of L.'s] legislative committee . . ." "declares that the Johnson . . ."
  See, for example, *San Bernardino Daily Sun*, March 31, 1924, p. 2.
"astronomical birth rate . . ." "increased landholding . . ." "They come here specifically
  and professedly . . ." "for the purposes of colonizing . . ." http://encyclopedia.densho
  .org/V.S._McClatchy/.
"Members of Japanese businesses and cultural organizations . . ." Loureiro, Pedro A.
  "Japanese Espionage and American Countermeasures in Pre-Pearl Harbor California."
  Journal of American-East Asian Relations, Vol. 3, No. 3 (Fall 1994), p. 200.
"In 1931 and 1934 . . ." Gripentrog, John. "The Transnational Pastime: Baseball and
  American Perceptions of Japan in the 1930s." *Diplomatic History*, Vol. 34, No. 2
  (April 2010), pp. 251–2.

CHAPTER 22: FEAR AND FICTION

"there was no danger of widespread anti-American activities . . ." "were in more danger
  from whites . . ." "The Nisei are pathetically eager . . ." https://www.digitalhistory
  .uh.edu/active_learning/explorations/japanese_internment/munson_report.cfm.
"A Jap is a Jap . . ." "There isn't such a thing as a loyal Japanese . . ." Muller, Eric.
  American Inquisition. The Hunt for Japanese American Disloyalty in World War II
  (Chapel Hill: University of North Carolina Press, 2007), p. 33.
"important installations" Cho, Sumi. "Redeeming Whiteness in the Shadow of Intern-
  ment: Earl Warren, Brown, and a Theory of Racial Redemption." *Boston College
  Third World Law Journal*, Vol. 19, No. 1 (December 1998), p. 92.
"The Japanese situation as it exists in California today . . ." Ibid.
"distribution of the Japanese population . . ." "ideally situated with reference to
  points . . ." Ibid., p. 94.
"We're charged with wanting to get rid . . ." Manzella, Abigail G. H. *Migrating Fictions:
  Gender, Race, and Citizenship in U.S. Internal Displacements* (Columbus: The Ohio
  State University Press, 2018), p. 116.

CHAPTER 23: NO ISLAND PARADISE

"Admiral Isoroku Yamamoto . . ." https://time.com/5802127/hawaii-internment-order/.
"At the Puna Hongwanji temple . . ." https://lithub.com/the-forgotten-internment-of
-japanese-americans-in-hawaii/.
"The Office of the Military Governor's official policy . . ." Ibid.

CHAPTER 24: INFAMY

"tar paper-covered barracks . . ." https://dp.la/exhibitions/japanese-internment
/home-family/.
"spare, prison-like compounds . . ." https://www.loc.gov/classroom-materials/immigration
/japanese/behind-the-wire/.
"Japanese Americans who cooperated . . ." Densho Encyclopedia. http://encyclopedia
.densho.org/Manzanar.
"They won seven Distinguished Unit Citation . . ." Ibid. https://encyclopedia.densho
.org/442nd_Regimental_Combat_Team/.

CHAPTER 25: FOUR WHO REFUSED

"I didn't feel guilty . . ." https://encyclopedia.densho.org/Korematsu_v._United_States/.
"whether, acting in cooperation . . ." 320 U.S. 81 (1943).
"extends to every matter and activity . . ." "tended to increase their isolation . . ." Ibid.
"a case of keeping people off the streets at night." 323 U.S. 214 (1944).
"All legal restrictions which curtail . . ." "We are not unmindful of the hardships . . ."
Ibid.
"the Court for all time has validated the principle of racial discrimination . . ." Ibid.
"I agreed to do it . . ." https://encyclopedia.densho.org/Mitsuye_Endo/.

EPILOGUE: SHAME

"he took the Colorado bar" https://encyclopedia.densho.org/Minoru_Yasui/.
"also fought discrimination beyond . . ." Ibid.
"deeply regretted the removal order . . ." Cray, Ed. *Chief Justice: A Biography of Earl
Warren* (New York, 1997: Simon & Schuster), p. 240.
"Donald Trump called Monday . . ." https://www.washingtonpost.com/news
/post-politics/wp/2015/12/07/donald-trump-calls-for-total-and-complete-shutdown
-of-muslims-entering-the-united-states/.
"*Korematsu* has nothing to do with this case . . ." 585 U.S. 38 (2018).
"In a manner very much akin to Roberts's opinion . . ." https://www.acslaw.org
/expertforum/trump-v-hawaii-and-chief-justice-robertss-korematsu-overruled
-parlor-trick/.

PHOTOGRAPH AND
ILLUSTRATION CREDITS

Photos ©: xiii: National Archives; 4: U.S. Senate Historical Office; 5: Library of Congress; 7: Library of Congress; 10: The Granger Collection; 14: National Archives; 16: The Huntington Library; 20: The Bancroft Library; 22–23: Wellcome Collection; 24: Library of Congress; 26: Pictures From History/age fotostock; 27: Library of Congress; 28–29: University of Southern California Libraries/California Historical Society; 31: Free Library of Philadelphia/Bridgeman Images; 32: The Granger Collection; 38: National Archives; 40: The Bancroft Library; 45: Library of Congress; 46: The Bancroft Library; 48: National Library of Medicine; 53: Labor Archives and Research Center, San Francisco State University; 54: San Francisco National Maritime National Historical Park; 57: San Francisco National Maritime National Historical Park; 59: The Bancroft Library; 60: The Bancroft Library; 66: University of California, Riverside; 69: Chinese Historical Society of America; 71: Chinese Historical Society of America; 73: Library of Congress; 75: Andriy Blokhin/Shutterstock; 87: University of California, Riverside; 96–97: Bettmann/Getty Images; 104–105: The Bancroft Library; 111: Library of Congress; 120: Courtesy of The Universal Message (www.mozumdar.org); 126–127: University of Washington/United States Government Printing Office; 130: Courtesy of the Harada Family Archival Collection/Museum of Riverside, Riverside, California; 133: Photography by Deborah Wong; 141: The Bancroft Library; 148: Japanese American National Museum (Gift of the Takeya Family, 99.208.1); 150: Library of Congress; 159: Library of Congress; 165: David Thind; 172: David Thind; 178–179: Japanese American Museum of Oregon; 180: Courtesy of the California History Room, California State Library, Sacramento, California; 182: Library of Congress; 183: Washington State Library; 188–189: Associated Press/AP Images; 194: The Bancroft Library; 196: Japanese Americans in World War II Collection, Special Collections Research Center, Henry Madden Library, California State University, Fresno; 201: National Archives; 202–203: Library of Congress; 206–207: Library of Congress; 208: Library of Congress; 211: University of Washington Libraries, Special Collections, UW36680; 213: National Portrait Gallery, Smithsonian Institution, gift of the daughters of Minoru Yasui; 214: Photo Courtesy of the Fred T. Korematsu Institute; 218: Library of Congress; 220–221: Utah State Historical Society.

INDEX

Page numbers in *italics* refer to illustrations.

Adams, John, 4
African Americans
    and citizenship, 7, 11, 13, 149,
        152
    Civil Rights Act of 1875, 17
    discrimination against, xiv, 43,
        109
    and Jim Crow rule, 181
    voting bans, 116
Ah Yup, 20, 117, 154, 161
alien land laws
    anti-Japanese legislation, 114–18,
        144–45
    and eligibility for citizenship,
        116–19, 157, 177–79
    and Harada family, 130–34
    legal challenges to, 176–80
    loopholes in, 122, 129, 175
    repeal of, 135
    in Washington, 174–77, 210
    and white supremacy, 144–45
Altmann, Aaron, 78–79, 142
American Civil Liberties Union,
        215
American Federation of Labor, 34,
        124
American Legion, 144
Army Corps of Engineers, 200
Arthur, Chester A., 23
Asian Americans
    and assimilation, xvi, 79, 114,
        169

considered nonwhite, 20–21,
        117, 169
    discrimination against, xiv–xvii,
        14, 19, 45, 63–64, 109
    and school segregation, 77–78
    See also Chinese Americans;
        Japanese Americans
Asiatic Barred Zone, 125, *126–27*

baseball, 186–87, *188–89*
Beck, James M., 157
Black, Hugo L., xii, 218, *218*,
        227–29
Blumenbach, Johann, 21, *22–23*,
        171
Boodle Boys, 68, 70, 84, 142
Brown v. Board of Education, 226
bubonic plague, 47–48, *48*, 49
Buchanan, James, 7
Buck v. Bell, xii
Burns, William J., 73, *73*, 74, 84
Butler, Pierce, 177–80

California
    alien land laws, 114–17, 157,
        178–79
    anti-Chinese laws in, 13, 15, 19,
        22–23
    anti-Japanese legislation,
        100–102
    Chinese and Japanese exclusion
        in, 47–48

California (*cont.*)
    Chinese immigration to, 9–13, 15
    and Gold Rush, 9–10
    Japanese immigration to, 30, 81
    tax on foreign miners, 10
California Federation of Labor, 144
California State Grange, 144
Cameron, Simon, 11
Carnegie, Andrew, 100
Casey, Michael, 52
Caucasians
    and naturalization, 161, 171
    as white persons, 12, 21, 114,
        157, 161, 164, 169–70
Chambers, John S., xvi
Chicago Columbian exposition of
    1893, 102
China
    American trade with, 70
    immigration to California, 9–11,
        13, 15
    Japanese occupation of, 185
    and Twenty-one Demands,
        137–38
    war with Japan, 81
Chinatown (San Francisco)
    Chinese architecture in, 74, *75*
    destroyed by fire and earthquake,
        67–68, *69*
    mass evictions from, 68–70
    rebuilding of, 70, 72–74
    relocation plans, 68–70, *71*
    and tourism, 70
    value of real estate to wealthy
        whites, 68–69
Chinese Americans
    acceptance of, 138
    and assimilation, 50, 114
    ban on citizenship, 20–21, 36–37

    ban on women immigrants,
        16–17
    and birthright citizenship,
        39–43
    discrimination against, 10,
        12–13, 15, 19, 22–23, *24*
    and Gold Rush, 9–10
    immigration ban, 23–24, 36
    legal challenges to
        discrimination, 15, 39–40, 50,
        70, 72
    as low-cost laborers, 10–11, 13,
        15, 17, 19, 33
    and naturalized citizenship,
        11–12, 18–22
    and Page Act, 16–17
    population rates, 11
    and voting rights, 12, 41–42
    as "white", 18–20
Chinese Consolidated Benevolent
    Association, 39–40, *40*
Chinese Exclusion Act, 23, 33, 50,
    158
Chinese Exclusion Convention, 64
*Citizens United v. Federal Election
    Commission*, xii
citizenship
    and African Americans, 7, 11, 13,
        149, 152
    birthright, xiv–xv, 36–37, 39–44,
        95
    and Chinese immigrants, 11–12,
        18–22, 36–37
    and enslaved people, 5–8
    for free whites, 3–4, 7–8, 11–12,
        16, 20–22, 117, 158–59,
        168–72
    and Japanese immigrants, 34–35,
        117–19, 132, 152, 155

jus sanguinis (law of the blood) theory, 37

jus soli (law of the soil) theory, 36–37, 41

and land ownership, 117–18, 177–78

opposition to multiracial, 12–13, 22

and U.S. Constitution, 1–2

and voting rights, 1–2, 4, 20, 41–42, 116–17

See also naturalization

City Front Federation, 53, 61

Civil Rights Act of 1875, 17

Clemons, Charles, 153–55, 162–63

Cleveland, Grover, 124

Committee for the Relocation of Chinese, 68

Conmy, Peter, 142–43

Coolidge, Calvin, 181, 184

Coronado National Forest, 224

Cox, James M., 145

Cronin, Daniel, 13

Cushman, Edward, 176

Davies, Vivian, *172*, 173

Dayal, Har, 167

democracy, 227–28, 230

Democrats, 62, 99, 108, 114–15

DeWitt, John, 193–95, 222–23, 227

discrimination

against African Americans, xiv, 43, 109

against Asian Americans, xiv–xvii, 19, 45

boycott of Asian American businesses, *14*

against Chinese immigrants, 10, 12–13, 15, 19

against Japanese immigrants, 34–35, 86, 107–9, 230

and U.S. Supreme Court, xviii, 8, 228–30

See also racism

Dole, James, 149

Dole, Sanford Ballard, 149–50, *150*, 151, 153

Dole Foods, 149

Douglas, William O., xii, 222

Dred Scott v. Sandford, xii, 6–8

Emmons, Delos, 198

Employers' Association, 53, 55–57, 62

Endo, Mitsuye, 212, 215, 219, *220–21*, 222, 226

Estudillo, Miguel, 133

Ex parte Endo, 222

Executive Order 589, 91

Executive Order 9066, xii, 195, 200, 210, 215, 222

Farm Bureau, 144

Federal Bureau of Investigation (FBI), 186, 191, 197

Federation of Women's Clubs, 144

Fifteenth Amendment, 12

Fifth Amendment, 8

442nd Regimental Combat Team, 208–9

Fourteenth Amendment, xv, 37, 40–43, 118, 145, 176, 179

Frick v. Webb, 180

Gage, Henry, 48

Gehrig, Lou, *188–89*

Gentlemen's Agreement, 92–93, 102, 106, 125
Ghadr Party, 166–67, 169
Gillett, James N., 102
Gogh, Vincent van, 30
Gold Rush, 9, *10*
Gompers, Samuel, 182, *182*, 227
Gotō Shinpei, xv
Grant, Ulysses, 17, 20, 31, *32*
Gray, Horace, 42–43
Great Britain, 123, 137
Grizzly Bear, 142–43
Gunnerson, Fulton, 129

Hamada family, *178–79*
Hamilton, Alexander, 1, 230
Harada, Harold, 135
Harada, Jukichi, 129, *130*, 131–35, 143
Harada, Sumi, 135
Harada House, *133*, 135
Harding, Warren G., 145
Hawaii
    Japanese American arrests and internment in, 197–99
    Japanese American citizenship in, 147, 149–55
    Japanese American combat regiments, 208, *208*, 209
    Japanese American community in, 30, 153, 198
    Japanese sugar plantation laborers in, 26–27, *28–29*, 30, 33
    martial law in, 198–99
    Pearl Harbor attack, xi, 190, 197
    surveillance of Japanese Americans, 198–99
Hawaiian Pineapple Company, 149

Hayes, Everis, 81
Hearst, William Randolph, *111*
    anti-Asian views of, 42, 47
    antipathy for Wilson, 112–13
    and Japanese fearmongering, 79, 82, 110, 112, 123, 138, 141, 162
    newspaper ownership, 47, 138, 141
    and Progressive movement, 110
    and white supremacy, 227
Heney, Francis J., 72–73, 84–85, 88, 116, 123
Hindu-German Conspiracy, 167
Hirabayashi, Gordon, 210, *211*, 212, 215–16, 218, 224–25
History of the American People (Wilson), 113
Hughes, Charles Evans, 156

immigration
    anti-Chinese laws, 15–19
    Asiatic Barred Zone, 125, *126–27*
    ban on Chinese, 16–17, 23–24, 36, 114
    ban on Japanese, 182, 184
    ban on Japanese laborers, 80, 90–93, 106–7, 125
    and birthright citizenship, 39–44
    and cheap labor, 10–11
    Chinese, 9–13, 15
    and citizenship, 11, 13, 16, 20, 22
    and Gold Rush, 9–10
    Japanese, 33–34, 51, 106
    and literacy test restriction, 124–25, 181
    and miner tax, 10

restrictions on Asian, xiv–xv,
125, 181–82, 184
and Trump administration ban,
229–30
US commercial and navigation
treaty with Japan, 106–7
Inman, James, 144
Inouye, Daniel, 209
Inui, Kiyo Sue, 76
Issei, 95, 195, 197

Jackson, Andrew, 7
Jackson, Robert, 219
Japan
annexation of Korea, 78, 137, 139
baseball in, 186–87, *188–89*
1876 Centennial exhibition,
30, *31*
exemption from restrictive
immigration law, 124–25
and expansionism, 136–38
and Gentlemen's Agreement,
90–92, 102, 125
influence on West, 30–31, 33
and insult of Japanese land
ownership ban, 101–2,
115–18, 121
Meiji Restoration, 26, 185
militarism in, 185–86
occupation of China, 185
Pearl Harbor attack, xi, 190–91
reception for Ulysses Grant,
31–32, *32*
rise of nationalism, 185
and school segregation crisis,
79–81, 88–90
Tokugawa shogunate, 25
and Twenty-one Demands,
137–38

US commercial and navigation
treaty with, 106–107
war with China, 81
and Western trade, 25, *26*, 30, 33
and World War I, 123, 136–38
Japan Society, 156
Japanese
contract labor in Hawaii, 26–27,
30, 33
demonizing of, 78–79, 81–82
exclusion of laborers, 90–93
immigration to California,
33–34
as "Mongolians", 118, 132, 150,
155
as "whites", 157, 160
Japanese American internment
children in, 205
concentration camp conditions,
200, 204–5, *206–7*
denial of due process, 212,
215–16, 222
and Hawaiian residents, 198–99
legal challenges to, 210, 212,
215–19, 222
loss of property, 204, 224
and mass relocations, 195–96,
200, *201*, 204
poster ordering evacuation, *xiii*
release of detainees, 223
Roosevelt's authorization for,
xi–xii, 195
Tule Lake internment camp,
202–3, 205, 219
Japanese Americans
and assimilation, xvi–xvii, 50–51,
79, 114, 187
ban on citizenship, 34–35,
117–19, 132, 155

Japanese Americans (*cont.*)
  ban on land ownership, 107–8,
    114–18, 122, 140, 145, 155,
    176–80
  and birthright citizenship, 95
  combat regiments, 208, *208*, 209
  discrimination against, xiv–xvii,
    34–35, 86, 185–86, 230
  exclusion advocacy, 47, 49–50,
    99, 143–46
  as farm laborers, 34, 98, 108, 115
  and farm ownership, 98, 106,
    108, 115, 122–23, 155, 175,
    178–79
  identification as Americans,
    184–85, 191
  landholdings in California, 108,
    115, 122, 124
  as low-cost laborers, 33–34
  loyalty to America, 191–92, *196*,
    198, 205, 208–10, 215–16
  naturalization rights, 147,
    149–54, 227
  and picture brides, 94–95,
    96–97, 144
  population rates, 95, 108,
    174–75, 184
  and school segregation, 77–80,
    90–91
  suspicion of sabotage, 186–87,
    191–92, 194–95, 197
Japanese and Korean Exclusion
  League, 86
Japanese Association of America,
  50–51, 79–80, 145–46
Japanese Associations of the Pacific
  Coast, 156
Japanese Exclusion League, 143–44
Jefferson, Thomas, 4

Johnson, Albert, 176
Johnson, James, 12
Johnson-Reed Act, 181–82, 184

Kalakaua, King, 26
Kearney, Denis, 13
Kearny Street battle, 61–62
Knights of Labor, 13
Korea, 78, 137, 139
Korean Americans, 77, 79
Korematsu, Fred T., *214*, 215–19,
  222, 225–26
Korematsu v. United States, xii, 8,
  222, 227, 229
Ku Klux Klan, 142, 218–19

Labor Council, 56
labor organizations
  and anti-immigration legislation,
    182
  and Asian exclusion, 50, 55,
    59, 63
  discrimination against the
    Chinese, 13, *14*, 17, 19, 23
  discrimination against the
    Japanese, *14*, 34–35, 82–83,
    100
  and increased competition, 100
  Kearny Street battle, 61–62
  Local 85, *53*
  negotiation for working
    conditions and pay, 52–53, 56
  and political candidates, 56–57
  and strikebreakers (scabs),
    55–56, *57*
  strikes by, 55–56, 61–62
  teamsters union, 52, 54–55
  threat of strikes, 52–55
  waterfront workers, 53, *54*

land ownership
    accusations of Japanese threat
        to white farmers, 107–8, 115,
        123
    alien land laws, 114–18, 144–45,
        175–76
    anti-Asian legislation, xiv, 128
    anti-immigrant legislation, 101
    anti-Japanese legislation, 107–8,
        114–16, 131, 140, 145,
        175–77
    and birthright citizens, 129, 134
    Chinese, 69–70, 73
    and citizenship, 117–18, 177–78
    by Japanese farmers, 98, 108,
        115, 155
    and race undesirability, 117
Langdon, William Henry, 84–85
Lawrence, John, 2
League of Nations, 145
Liliuokalani, Queen, 149
Look Tin Eli, 74, 75

Maclay, William, 4, 4
Madison, James, 2–3
Marshall, James, 9
McClatchy, V. S.
    and Japanese exclusion, 47,
        138–39, 144, 182, 183, 184
    newspaper ownership, 47, 138,
        141, 143–44, 182
    and white supremacy, 141,
        143–44, 227
McDougald, John E., 142
McNab & Smith, 52
Meiji, Emperor of Japan, 25–26, 27,
    30, 32
Meiji Restoration, 26, 185
Metcalf, Victor, 81–82

Mikado, The, 30
Missouri Compromise, 6, 8
"Mongolians"
    ban on voting rights, 12
    Chinese as, 118
    Japanese as, 118, 132, 150, 155
    and naturalization, 12, 18
    as not white, 20–22, 154
    and race theory, 21
    and school segregation, 78
Morgan, J. P., 100
Morton, Oliver, 12
Mozumdar, Akhay Kumar, 119,
    120, 161, 166, 168, 172
Murphy, Frank, 219
Muslims, 228–29

Nakatsuka, N., 175–77
Native Daughters of the Golden
    West, 141–42, 144
Native Sons of the Golden West,
    141, 141, 142–44
naturalization
    and African Americans, 11, 13,
        149, 162
    and Chinese exclusion, 11, 18,
        23, 33, 50, 158
    and citizenship, 2–3, 119
    and Hindus, 164, 166–69
    and Japanese immigrants, 147,
        149–54, 227
    law of 1790, 3–4, 11, 22
    and military service, 173
    of "Mongolians", 12, 18
    residency requirement, 2–4
    for whites, 4, 11–12, 16, 149,
        161–62, 166, 171
Naturalization Act (1790), 3–4, 11,
    149, 152, 157–59

Ng Poon Chew, 70
Nisei, 95, 123, 184–85, 197, 199
Northwest American Japanese
    Association, 176

Obama, Barack, 224–25
Office of Naval Intelligence (ONI),
    186, 191, 197
Older, Fremont, 72, 88
Ozawa, Takao, *148*
    citizenship appeal, 155–58
    denial of citizenship, 154
    education and background, 147
    petition for citizenship, 147,
        149–54
    Supreme Court denial for
        citizenship, 158–62, 169–71
Ozawa v. United States, 157

Page, Horace, 15–16, *16*, 17, 19,
    22–23, 227
Page Act, 16–18
Panama-Pacific International
    Exposition
    grounds of, *104–5*
    Japanese pavilion in, 103,
        106, 121
    Japanese support for, 115,
        117–18, 121
    showcasing of San Francisco,
        102–3
Pearl Harbor attack, xi, 190–91,
    197, 228
Perry, Matthew, 25, *26*
Phelan, James Duval, *45, 46*
    and alien land laws, 114–15, 117,
        145–46
    anti-Asian views of, xv–xvi, 45,
        47–48, 50–51, 63–64, 99, 106

anti-Japanese views, 117–18,
    121, 124–25, 139–40,
    162, 182
anti-union sentiment, 55–56
and ban on Japanese land
    ownership, 107–8, 140
elected as mayor of San
    Francisco, 47
elected to Senate, 122–23
formation of Japanese Exclusion
    League, 143–44
quarantine of Chinatown and
    Japantowns, 48–49
as San Francisco socialite, 45–46
and white supremacy, 45, 47, 51,
    139–42, 227
and Wilson's views on immigrant
    labor, 113–14
picture brides, 94–95, *96–97*,
    144, 182
Plessy v. Ferguson, xii, xv, 42–43
Porterfield v. Webb, 178
Presidential Medal of Freedom,
    225–26
Progressive movement, 99–100,
    109–10

racism
    and African Americans, 43, 109,
        113, 181
    anti-Asian, 45, 48, 109, 175
    and anti-Chinese citizenship, 12
    and anti-Chinese immigration,
        13, *24*, 30
    and citizenship eligibility, 162–63
    and Japanese American
        internment, 219
    and Japanese American students,
        86, 90, 143

and Japanese exclusion, 99, 139,
142, 184–86
and Japanese land ownership,
115, 177
persistence of, 227–30
and U.S. Supreme Court,
xvii–xviii, 8, 180, 227–30
See also discrimination; white
supremacy
Republicans, 62, 106–7, 109
Riordan, Thomas, 40–41
Roberts, John, 228–29
Roberts, Owen, 217, 219
Rockefeller, John D., 100
Roosevelt, Franklin
declares war on Japan, xi, 191
and Japanese American
internment, xi–xii, 195,
198, 200
suspicion of Japanese Americans,
186, 193–94, 197
Roosevelt, Theodore
and Gentlemen's Agreement,
90–92, 102
investigation into Ruef and
Schmitz, 72–73
and Japanese relations, 82,
88–92, 136, 143
and Japan-Russia peace treaty, 89
opposition to anti-Japanese
legislation, 101–2
and Progressive movement, 100,
109–10
Schmitz delegation to, 89–90
and school segregation crisis,
80–82, 88–90
Root, Elihu, 80–81, 102, 156
Ross, Edward A., 50
Royal Order of Moose, 144

Ruef, Abraham, *59*
and city workers, *63*
corrupt activities of, 62–64, 72,
74, 76, 85–86
education and background, 58
eviction of Chinese from
Chinatown, 68–70
indictment for extortion, 86, 88
investigation into, 73–74, 76,
84–86
and San Francisco politics,
58–59, 61–62
targeting of Japanese, 76–79
and the Union Labor Party, 59
Russo-Japanese War, 78, 89
Ruth, Babe, *188–89*

Sacramento Bee, 143–44, 182
San Francisco
anti-Chinese laws in, 13
bubonic plague in, 47–49
exclusion advocacy in, 47, 49–51
and Gold Rush boom, 9–10
labor unions in, 47, 49–50
labor unrest in, 52–57, 61–62
opposition to anti-Japanese
legislation, 102–3
Panama-Pacific International
Exposition, 102–3, *104–5*, 106
political machine in, 58
population rates, 9
quarantine of Chinatown and
Japantowns, 48–49
Six Companies in, 39–40, 50
San Francisco earthquake (1906),
65, *66*, 67–69
San Francisco Examiner, 79, 82,
110, 112, 115, 123, 139,
145, 162

Sanitary Act (1870), 13
Sawyer, Lorenzo, 20, *20*, 21–22
Schmitz, Eugene E., *60*
  corrupt activities of, 62–64,
    72–74, 76
  election as mayor of San
    Francisco, 61–62
  and eviction of Chinese, 69
  indictment for extortion, 86,
    88–89
  investigation into, 84–85
  loyalty of city workers, 63
  meeting with Teddy Roosevelt,
    87, 89–91
  targeting of Japanese, 78, 86
  and white supremacy, 142
school segregation
  Brown v. Board of Education,
    226–27
  as insult to Japan, 79–81, 88–89
  Roosevelt's response to, 80–82
  and targeting of Japanese, 77–81,
    90
Scott, Dred, 5, *5*, 6
Scott, Harriet Robinson, 5, *5*, 6
Scudder, Doremus, 155
Shortridge, Samuel, 145
Sing Chong Bazaar, 74
Six Companies, 39, *40*, 50, 69–70
slavery, 6–8
Spreckels, Rudolph, 72–73
Stanford, Leland, 20
Stilwell, Joseph W. "Vinegar Joe,"
    193
Stone, Harlan Fiske, 217, 227
Sumner, Charles, 11, 22
Sutherland, George, *159*
  on citizenship and assimilation,
    171–72

and constitutional definition of
    white, 158–61, 164, 169–71
  and Ozawa citizenship denial,
    158, 160–61, 172
  and Thind citizenship denial,
    170–72
Sutter, John, 9

Taft, Howard, 101–2, 106, 109,
    124, 136, 156, 158
Taliaferro, Lawrence, 5
Taney, Roger Brooke, 6–7, *7*, 8
Terrace, Elizabeth, 175–76, 178
Terrace, Frank, 175–76, 178
Thind, Bhagat Singh, 164, *165*,
    166–71, *172*, 173
Thomas, Clarence, 43
Thompson, J. Wesley, 153
Thompson, Lindsay, 176
Tobin, Joseph, 62
Tokugawa shogunate, 25
Truman, Harry, 209
Trumbull, Lyman, 12
Trump, Donald, 228–30
Trump v. Hawaii, 228–29
Tsutsumi, Kenneth, 226
Tule Lake internment camp,
    202–3, 205, 219
Twenty-one Demands, 137–38

Union Labor Party, 57, 59, 76
United Commercial Bank (San
    Francisco), *75*
United States v. Wong Kim Ark,
    42–43, 45
U.S. Constitution, xi, 1–2
U.S. Supreme Court
  and alien land laws, 176–80
  Brown v. Board of Education, 226

discrimination by, xviii, 8, 180, 228–30

Dred Scott v. Sandford, 6–8

Ex parte Endo, 222

and Japanese American internment, xi–xii, 216–19, 222, 224

Korematsu v. United States, xii, 8, 222, 227, 229

Ozawa citizenship petition, 156–62, 169–71

Plessy v. Ferguson, 42–43

Porterfield v. Webb, 178

Thind citizenship petition, 169–71

Trump v. Hawaii, 228–29

United States v. Wong Kim Ark, 42–43, 45

Webb v. O'Brien, 180

US commercial and navigation treaty with Japan, 106–7

Van Reed, Eugene, 27

voting rights
and birthright citizens, 39, 41
and citizenship, 1–2, 4, 20, 41–42, 116–17
for free whites, 12
and property ownership, 1

Warren, Earl, 142, 193–94, *194*, 195, 226–27

Washington
alien land laws, 157, 174–77
anti-Asian laws in, 174–75
anti-Japanese legislation, 101, 175–77
Japanese population in, 174–75

Washington, George, 3–4, 160

Webb, Ulysses, *180*
anti-Japanese views, 162
attempt to seize Harada home, 131–34
enforcement of alien land law, 128
on property rights and citizenship, 116–17
on threat of Japanese farmers, 115, 122, 124
and white supremacy, 142, 227

Webb v. O'Brien, 180

Wells, Asa, 62

Whistler, James Abbott McNeill, 30

white supremacy
anti-Chinese views, 39
anti-immigration legislation, 181
anti-Japanese legislation, 100–101
anti-Japanese views, 136–37, 140–42, 186, 196
ban on African American voting rights, 116
ban on Japanese American land ownership, 107–8, 116–17, 176
discrimination against Asian Americans, xiv–xv, xvii, 47
and Progressive movement, 100
and school segregation, 79
See also racism

whites
anti-Japanese views, 143
as Caucasians, 21, 161, 164, 169–71
Chinese as, 18–20
and citizenship, 3–4, 7–8, 11–12, 16, 20–22, 117–19, 168–72

whites (*cont.*)
  Japanese as, 157, 160
  legal definition of, 21–22, 119,
      154, 160–61, 164, 169–71
  "Mongolians" as not, 20–22, 154
  skull size and shape, 21, *22–23*
  threat of Chinese to, 17, 39
Wickersham, George, 156–58
Wilson, Woodrow
  anti-immigrant views, 113–14
  as Democratic presidential
      candidate, 107–9, 113–14
  election as president, 114
  favorable views of Chinese, 113
  Hearst attacks on, 112–13
  History of the American People,
      113
  and immigration literacy test
      restriction, 124–25
  and Japanese American land
      ownership ban, 116
  League of Nations, 145
  racist views on African
      Americans, 109, 113
  and World War I, 123
Wolverton, Charles, 167–68
Wong Ah Yee, 19

Wong Kim Ark, 37, *38*, 39–43, 94
Workingmen's Party of California,
    13
World War I
  alignment of Japan and Great
      Britain, 123, 137
  Japanese allies in, 123, 136–37
  Japanese ultimatum with China,
      137–38
World War II
  arrest of Japanese Americans,
      191, 195–97
  Battle of Midway, 197–98
  Japanese American combat
      regiments, 208, *208*, 209
  Pearl Harbor attack, xi, 190–91,
      197, 228
  suspicion of Japanese Americans,
      186–87, 191–94
  See also Japanese American
      internment
Wright, Luke, 80–81, 88–90

Yamamoto, Isoroku, 197–98
Yasui, Minoru "Min," 212, *213*,
    215–16, 218, 222, 225
Yates, Richard, 12

ACKNOWLEDGMENTS

I'd like to again thank Scholastic, especially David Levithan, Ellie Berger, and the late Dick Robinson, for their commitment to my work and for agreeing that history can be every bit as suspenseful and compelling as the best fiction. Lisa Sandell remains an editor so superb that I have to pinch myself to know she's real. Lizette Serrano and Emily Heddleson are a joy to work with, and Charlie Olsen at InkWell Management is a true partner. And, finally, my wife, Nancy; daughter, Lee; and son-in-law, Tyler, who seem willing to pretend that I'm easy to get along with.

ABOUT THE AUTHOR

Lawrence Goldstone is the critically acclaimed author of *Stolen Justice: The Struggle for African American Voting Rights*, which *School Library Journal* declared in a starred review: "A must-buy for all high school collections"; *Unpunished Murder: Massacre at Colfax and the Quest for Justice*, which *Booklist*'s starred review called "gripping . . . and a well-informed perspective on American history"; and *Separate No More: The Long Road to* Brown v. Board of Education, of which *Kirkus Reviews* said, "The prose is engaging and accessible for young readers without being condescending, and intense scenes from history illuminate nearly every chapter. Goldstone underlines the tireless efforts of civil rights activists despite staggering odds, offering hope for a present that is also plagued by racial inequalities and violence . . ." in its starred review. He is also the author of more than a dozen books for adults, including four on constitutional law. He lives in San Diego with his wife, medieval and Renaissance historian Nancy Goldstone.